BECOMING UNSTOPPABLE:

The Playbook for Creatives and Entrepreneurs

DANI FELT

Publishing Coach: Heather Andrews

Editor: Manita Sanoria Ramos

Photographer: Kidtee Hello Photography

Paperback Print ISBN: 979-8-218-94826-9

Hardcover Print ISBN: 979-8-218-94827-6

Printed in the United States of America

TABLE OF CONTENTS

DEDICATION

I want to dedicate this book to my family and friends.

TESTIMONIALS

"Dani Felt is a mover and shaker in the music industry. She has an uncanny ability to spot talent and turn big ideas into real momentum. Her passion, work ethic, and influence make her someone that artists and executives alike trust and follow."

– Adonis Tsilimparis, Composer

-oOo-

"Dani Felt is a visionary artist and entrepreneur who bridges music, PR, and storytelling to build meaningful connections between artists and audiences. With a sharp instinct for creative direction and market positioning, she transforms artistic identity into scalable, impactful business opportunities within the modern music landscape."

– Evan Stein

-oOo-

"Dani is relentless in the best possible way. Whether it's working on a show, a song, or for a client, she believes in the vision with every part of who she is. She dreams it, she sees it before it materializes, and she pursues every possible avenue and opportunity until the breakthrough happens. I've watched her go after something for years and years, while most others would have given up long ago.

Everyone needs a Dani to remind them to keep going."

– Robert Biehn

-oOo-

"Dani is an enterprising entrepreneur with a keen sense of the art life and how to live it. We need more Dani's in the world!"

– Dylan Berry

-oOo-

"Dani found her way into my world through one of my secret offers… and wow, what a gift! Her energy and heart are truly incredible. She's not just an artist in what she creates, she lives her artistry. The way she guides others back to their own creative truth is honest, embodied, and powerful.

Dani is the real deal. The world is brighter because she shares her magic."

– Jasmine Marra (Quantum Femme Wealth)

-oOo-

"Dani is a go-getter powerhouse in the music industry. She opens pathways where before there was just an endless forest. A great asset to any artist or team."

– Nicole de la Cruz

"Dani is extremely knowledgeable in the indie music world, having been an artist first before management skills."

– Steve Owens

-oOo-

"As a full-time indie artist, working with Dani Felt has been a game changer. She knows how to get music in front of the right audience and that's made all the difference."

– Ian Keller (Orphan Prodigy)

-oOo-

"Dani Felt is the most magnetic person I've ever met. She is a breath of fresh air radiating positivity, and improves the lives of everyone she meets. Nobody does networking and connecting like her; she's a prime example of being able to do anything you put your mind to. She can make a friend, host a successful event, and change a life anywhere. I'd recommend everyone to follow her example and take her advice!"

– Brina Kay

-oOo-

"One of my favorite things about Dani is her passion, creativity, and relentless drive to bring light to the world through everything she does. She is a natural connector with an intuitive ability to see talent, amplify voices, and build relationships that genuinely move the music industry forward.

Dani works hard, but more importantly, she works with heart and a deep respect for the artists and people she supports. She's the kind of woman who doesn't just chase success, she elevates everyone in the room while doing it!"

– Kat Cozadd

"Working with Dani, what stood out for me most was her genuine heart for service. She truly cares about people and the impact of the work she puts into the world. She is a deeply collaborative person who is excellent at bringing creatives together and supporting them in the exact ways they need.

She doesn't shy away from limitations, but instead, I saw her continue to play a bigger and bigger game. Dani brings a dedication to creativity and helping others move forward. This book is going to be an incredible resource for anyone wanting to create more alignment and stop feeling limited. Congrats, Dani!"

– Christy Avis

FOREWORD

In the arena of life, there is a pattern that becomes impossible to ignore.

I've seen it play out late at night in recording studios, in high-stakes business negotiations, and in the pressure-filled cycles behind fast-growing brands and top-tier influencers.

Across platforms, industries, and business models, most people do not stall because they lack talent. They stall because their internal operating system cannot support the level of opportunity they are pursuing. When pressure increases, cracks appear. Strategy loses coherence. Momentum fades. What follows is often labeled bad luck, when it is usually something far more predictable.

Becoming Unstoppable is not a book about tactics in isolation. It is a book about the internal structure required to execute any strategy consistently, sustain progress under pressure, and follow through when momentum starts to test character. Without that structure, even the best ideas eventually collapse under their own weight.

Anyone who has spent time building something real has seen this play out. Two people can be given the same advice, the same resources, and the same opportunities, yet produce very different outcomes. The difference is rarely intelligence or effort. It shows up in standards, in tolerance for discomfort, and in the decisions made when no one is watching.

This is Dani Felt's battleground.

There are many ways to engage with this book, depending on what you need at this stage of your journey. Some readers may experience it as a mindset shift. Others may see it as a recalibration of identity, discipline, or direction. Some may move through it slowly, reflecting on each chapter. Others may recognize patterns they have already lived and move quickly.

What remains consistent is the underlying truth running through it all. Sustainable growth requires alignment. Progress accelerates when decisions, values, and actions stop working against one another. The ideas in this book are not positioned as guarantees. They function as frameworks for how people operate under pressure. They influence behavior. They clarify boundaries. Over time, those choices compound.

When Dani speaks about alignment, she is pointing to the reduction of internal friction. When she speaks about self-worth, she is addressing decision quality. When she speaks about energy, she is speaking to sustainability and the ability to show up consistently without self-sabotaging when momentum arrives.

I have watched people implode the moment success finally showed up because their internal framework was not built to hold it. I have also watched others grow steadily, not because they chased every new tactic, but because they built a grounded sense of direction that made their actions repeatable and resilient.

Dani's perspective comes from proximity to that reality. She has spent years navigating real stakes. Money. Visibility. Rejection. Growth. Responsibility. The clarity in this book does not come from theory. It comes from repetition and pattern recognition.

This book asks something of the reader.

It asks for honesty.
It asks for ownership.
It asks for a willingness to examine habits, assumptions, and standards.

Some ideas may feel immediately familiar. Others may surface discomfort. That tension is not accidental. Growth rarely arrives gently. It tends to demand clarity, responsibility, and follow-through.

This is not a manual to be rushed through. It is a conversation to be engaged with. Take what resonates. Sit with what challenges you. Pay attention to resistance. That is often where the most meaningful work begins.

If you sense that the real constraint on your growth is not information, but alignment.

If you are ready to stop waiting for confidence and start acting with intention.

If you are prepared to raise the standards you live by, this book will meet you where you are.

Then it will demand more of you.

Growth always does. Welcome to the arena.

– Dallas Jack,
Founder of Spade Creative

About Spade Creative:

Today, Spade Creative is more than a studio. It's a team and a process, built around the belief that creativity is most powerful when it's holistic. We still chase the perfect take, but we also build the platforms, campaigns, and digital experiences that make those moments matter. What began as passion has grown into partnership with artists, businesses, and organizations who trust us to bring their vision to life in ways that last.

Connect with Dallas today at: www.spadecreative.org or scan the QR code below. Mention the code "Champion" for a free consultation.

INTRODUCTION

Music has been the heartbeat of my life for as long as I can remember. I was singing before I could even form full sentences. At two years old, I was belting out melodies in my childhood home. By age ten, I was taking voice lessons. Summers meant performance camps, where I lived for the thrill of being on stage.

But in middle school, everything changed. I was bullied, teased, and excluded in ways that cut deeply. It was painful, and at times I felt invisible. But instead of shutting down, I turned to writing. Poetry became my outlet, a way to pour out the emotions I didn't know how to express out loud. Eventually, those poems turned into songs. What had once been a private escape became a source of healing and, in time, empowerment. That's when I truly realized the power of music: It wasn't just about performance. It was about transformation.

When I was fourteen, I found myself in a recording studio for the first time. The hum of the equipment, the glow of the red light, the sound of my voice echoing back through the headphones, it was intoxicating. I thought, *"This is it. This is where I belong."*

Of course, the road from that starry-eyed teenager to where I am today was anything but smooth. After graduating college, I auditioned for "The Voice." I didn't make it, but the experience planted a seed.

I needed to put myself out there, no matter how scary or uncertain the outcome. Shortly after came one of the most pivotal moments of my career: an internship at a PR firm in London. I thought it would be glamorous, a stepping stone into the industry. Instead, I got fired.

At the time, it felt humiliating. But in hindsight, it was the spark I needed. That rejection lit a fire in me. I started a music blog as part passion project, part act of rebellion. That blog went on to feature over 300 interviews with artists and industry insiders, building connections I could never have dreamed of at the time.

I moved to New York City where I established a consulting agency with a partner, and when that partnership crumbled, I had a new beginning back home in Pennsylvania. I launched online courses like "Mindset Mastery" and "Network Like a Boss," where I taught artists the very lessons I was learning about manifestation and connection.

But I wasn't finished reinventing myself. Nashville called. Within a month of visiting, I had packed up and moved there. Nashville gave me five years of growth, music, and entrepreneurship. I launched my music marketing company, co-created a TV pilot that attracted producers, recorded my first commercial single "Queen" in 2019, and later released "Unapologetic" with my first music video in 2022. I also dove deep into spiritual courses to learn about energy, manifestation, and alignment; lessons that reshaped not only my career, but my life.

Of course, there were plenty of storms. Partnerships that fell apart. Burnout. Times when I didn't know how I was going to move forward. But every heartbreak became a lesson. Every misstep taught me resilience, self-love, and the importance of trusting my own voice above all else.

In 2024, I launched the PR division of my company. But in 2025, I got the nudge from my intuition: *There's nothing left for you in Nashville.*

It was time to leap again. This time to Los Angeles. Within months, I manifested a new home, new collaborations, and a new chapter. Now, I run my own PR, branding, and marketing agency and share my experiences through speaking, teaching, and my podcast.

Looking back, my journey feels like a movie, full of chaos, inspiration, betrayal, heartbreak, reinvention, and triumph. But it all traces back to those days of being bullied, when I discovered how powerful creativity could be as a tool for survival and self-expression. That was the seed that grew into everything I've built today.

And that's why I wrote this book.

This book is for the artist who doesn't know where to start, the entrepreneur who's tired of spinning their wheels, the dreamer who knows they're meant for more but isn't sure how to get there. If you've ever struggled with not knowing how to network, how to price your work, how to attract money, or how to even believe in yourself, then this book is for you.

Inside, you'll discover how to:

- Build stronger relationships and surround yourself with the right people.

- Get clear on your vision, your offers, and your pricing.

- Create a roadmap for your career or business.

- Spot red flags and avoid toxic partnerships.

- Attract money and opportunities using universal laws.

- Strengthen your leadership and self-trust.

- Embrace mistakes as part of the process.

- Step into your power and cultivate real self-love.

This book was born from years of emails and newsletters I sent to my community, each one a piece of my journey, a lesson learned, a truth uncovered. Looking back, I realize they weren't just reflections. They were a guide. A toolkit. A way to help others leap further, faster, without stumbling over the same roadblocks I did.

My mission is simple: To empower you to take action, no matter how small. Because those small steps? They add up. They change everything. They create momentum that carries you toward your dreams.

So if you're ready to stop waiting and start building, and finally claim the life and career you deserve, this book is your invitation.

This is your story now. This is your moment. Let's build your empire together.

Chapter 1

Fuck Perfection (Seriously, Let It Go)

I have been so challenged to try things outside of my comfort zone when it comes to being an artist. I have been getting really pushed to my limits, like trying to topline. I have tried to write over ten songs of toplining melodies. But then I started teaming up with people who topline and this comes so easily to them. My thing is lyrics. Everyone has their own thing.

As artists, we are so often told to be perfect. To have perfect social media numbers, be an incredible performer, sell lots of music, have perfect merch, be incredible in the studio, be an amazing topliner, lyricist, play all instruments, blah, blah, blah. I am here to tell you: IT IS SAFE TO NOT BE PERFECT. Drop the perfection act and play to your strengths. Team up with people who are good at what comes hard to you. This whole pretending to be perfect thing is super exhausting and I would much rather see you thrive.

It is safe to not be perfect. It is safe to have weaknesses. It is safe to ask for help and admit you need guidance on something. We are human and divine, but not perfect! Forgive yourself for what is not your best skills, and find people to team up with who are amazing with those things you struggle with. You will feel so much better.

Also try to be less harsh on yourself. Love yourself more, forgive yourself more. Your imperfection is a beautiful thing! It is okay to not have a great day, week, or month. Do what you gotta do. Be kind to yourself. YOU ARE AMAZING JUST THE WAY YOU ARE. Just be you!

Why do we always put so much pressure on ourselves to complete everything so perfectly? Why do we feel that art always has to be perfect? What happened to giving ourselves space, time, and magic to act on divine timing and know that it does not have to be perfect to be great? Can we, for once, start to enjoy the process and let go of rushing into everything? Can we learn to have more fun and enjoy the process of creating? Instead of wanting it to be perfect and never releasing it because we do not feel it is good enough. Can we just slow down a bit and breathe in the magic, and let go of some of the weights we put on ourselves day by day?

This was the reminder I got when I took a mini road trip to Ashland City to meet with a dear friend I have not seen in over five years. This girl is very special to me; we have so much history. She even performed at my book release party in New York City. When I stepped into her home, I felt such a warm, welcoming energy, such a good vibe. I saw plants everywhere, beautiful lighting, and amazing interior design. I felt like I was on vacation and it was just what my soul needed.

The trip was amazing! My friend is just a pure, kind-hearted person. She treated me to such delicious home-cooked meals. We had the most amazing songwriting session and heart-to-heart conversations. Her home is surrounded by trees and it felt so good to just be surrounded by nature. My soul felt so happy! Sometimes, we all just need to slow down and take a mental break.

Oh by the way, one crucial thing I did at this time was I turned my phone off for almost the entire day. It felt so good being disconnected from everyone and just focusing on being in the moment with my friend for our writing session. I highly recommend everyone to start taking more breaks from your phone. It led me to some powerful downloads and insights.

I also noticed that day, I felt more at peace because I barely looked at my social media. I think social media can really trigger a lot of anxiety in me, and hence, I'm trying to use it less. I think the biggest thing it does is lead me to constantly compare myself to everyone else's "perfect" life and what they are doing. That is actually not healthy and can cause a lot of insecurity, at least in my experience. So I vow to try to use social media less, except when posting, and focus more on staying in a state of peace. Really being in a peaceful state of mind is where we can manifest the fastest and most powerful, anyway.

When I asked my friend about the plans for her music, she told me she is working on an EP/album and that she is taking her time with it. She is not rushing to finish it so fast because she would rather have an amazing quality than rush just to get songs out. I loved this way of thinking and decided I will start to adapt this into my everyday way of being. Why rush? Why not enjoy it? Why not really appreciate where we are in the moment versus trying to always rush into the future and accomplish every single thing in an instant?

As an artist, I have felt pressured to release music every four to eight weeks, and honestly, that is a lot. I would rather be at peace and take my time than be in a state of constant stress and pressure. Maybe that is just me.

When I was working towards releasing my single "Unapologetic," I asked so many different producers their opinion of the song. I just could not part ways with it. It was never complete in my opinion. I could have mixed it over and over again. Being an artist, I can be quite the perfectionist. I just wanted it perfect. But you know what? I had to learn to let it go. To surrender the process. To give it up to God and the universe. To tell myself it is complete.

As an artist, as a creator, we can always keep editing but this is also a form of self-sabotage. We must learn to trust, let go, and surrender to the process of creating art. Music is subjective anyway, and it will never sound perfect. We can never please everyone! So learn to just embrace the imperfections of art and find harmony within yourself to enjoy the process!

Aim for Greatness

One New Year's Eve, I was really excited to go out and have fun, and see one of my friends perform live. I was on some kind of sugar high, not paying attention while I was doing laundry. I walked into my laundry room and suddenly bent down then straightened back up, and banged my head on the laundry dryer door which I forgot was not closed. If I was being more present, if I was in less of a rush, and paid more attention to the moment, maybe that would not have happened.

My long-winded point is maybe we just need to start to take our time more and take the pressure off ourselves. So what if something does not turn out as perfect as we wanted it to? Sometimes, things are going to be messy and we are going to make mistakes. If life was about perfection, gosh, we would all be so bored! Although sometimes, the project takes longer because the original idea is just not aligned anymore.

A great example: I had been working on my TV show for almost five years. It is absolutely not perfect. In fact, I have probably come up with at least nine to ten different versions of the show. But when it comes to creating, it's about development, it's about making it better and better. It is not about wanting it to be perfect, but it is about creating something great! So take off your "perfection lens," and instead, replace it with the "lens of greatness." Take it one scene at a time, one line at a time, one story at a time.

Why are we in a constant state of "this project needs to happen right now or else?" Why does it need to be perfect? That song you did might not be perfect, but it could be on its way to greatness! Take your time and just put in a beautiful intention for the song. Do not rush it. It does not need to be perfect. Just keep working on it until it is great. That book you are sitting on? Start writing it! That business plan you are dreaming of, start drafting it. Do not wait until something is perfect to get started on it. Just go forward and take action!

Also, let's start to look at things differently. Can we shift our mindset to: Projects will be done when they are meant to, that it is not about perfection but that divine timing is always at play.

Can we normalize just living in joy and embracing the messiness of life rather than being so damn critical of ourselves all the time? Life is not about perfection! It is about the experience—the good, the bad, the ugly—it is all for us to build our journey. This is the blessing of being human, not being perfect. Can we make a conscious effort to just enjoy life more and live in the moment versus acting in a constant state of fear and lack?

Can we start to adapt the mindset of "if not now, another time." If not this one person to work with my team, another one. If this singer will not record one of my songs, then another. If we cannot release our EP this month, then another month. If not this client, another one. A better-fitting client. A better-fitting singer. A better-fitting person to pitch xyz, or manage us, etc.

Rejection

I got rejected from The Recording Academy and I want you to know that rejection is a common part of being in this music world. It is part of being an artist, a producer, or just working in this industry, in general. It might hurt my feelings but at the same time, I believe that everything happens for a reason. If something is meant for us, it will be for us.

I want you to know, no matter how many doors get slammed in your face, you will be okay! And I want to encourage you to keep going no matter what. Keep trying, keep putting yourself out there, keep applying to every opportunity your heart desires. What's meant for you will align for you. Maybe someone else needed the membership more than me and that's okay. Sure, my ego might be like, how dare they not choose me! (You know what I mean, our ego can be a bit wild.) But my soul is like, it's okay and what is meant for me will be for me.

Never let an opportunity determine your worthiness. You are worthy of just being born. Never think that if you do not get an opportunity, or get into a certain label or management company that you are less worthy than a peer in your community of music friends. I shared this story to encourage you and to let you know, you got this. Do not be so hard on yourself when you do not always hear a "yes" in this fun music world. Keep going, keep going, keep going, keep going, keep going, and keep going. You are talented and an amazing human. The world needs your music no matter what. We need your creativity, inspiration, voice, etc.

Energy

The reason people will hire you as a coach, consultant, or artist; or buy your merch, go to your shows, or become a fan or client of yours is because they feel good about being around you. They love your energy and who you are. Let's be real, there are millions of artists out there. So, what makes people purchase from you or become a raving fan? It comes down to the quality of your offer, your brand awareness, and who you are as a human being. Your energy, your personality, your essence are the reasons people hire you, or buy your products or services, or become a super fan.

I got this realization when I asked some of my clients what their favorite part of my three-month program was and they said my energy and attitude. :) Then it hit me, it is not about being perfect, it is about being ourselves.

So take a deep breath, take the pressure off yourself and realize that the people who purchase from you are the people who love you for who you are—your attitude, your energy. Even your music resonates with a certain energy. Really take that in! You get to be paid for just being yourself. How beautiful is that?! It is not about being perfect, it is about being YOU. Although, do not get me wrong, if you are a producer, you do need to nail that mix or as an artist nail that recording. But at the end of the day, people hire us for being us!

Key Takeaways

1. Take mental breaks, surround yourself with nature, and surround yourself with things that inspire you.

2. Sometimes when you remove yourself from your current environment, you start to see a different perspective and get new insights, ideas, and creative thoughts that you never would have otherwise.

3. Slow down and enjoy the present moment more.

4. Take breaks from your phone and social media.

5. Be less harsh on yourself and just enjoy the process more than focusing so much on the destination of whatever it is you're trying to accomplish.

6. Take care of yourself, get enough sleep, and eat healthy. Make sure you have energy to do the things you want to do.

7. Take it one step at a time.

8. Really get clear on what you want in your life, not what others tell you is good for you. You want to be a signed artist, great! Go for it. You want to do more songwriting behind the scenes, that is okay too. There is no wrong or right answer. It is ultimately your life and you have to choose what is best for you!

Affirmations

- I am perfect just the way I am.

- My mistakes become my biggest power-ups in life.

- Being human is my gift and blessing.

- This or better always.

This Chapter Is Sponsored By

Tzayla
www.tzayla.com

Chapter 2

Messy Isn't Failure, It's Training

We all make mistakes. But, ask yourself, was it really a "mistake" or a lesson? You see, in life, we are given many opportunities to make decisions. That is the power of free will. Every single decision we make will create a different outcome.

For example, if you decide to go food shopping at 8 a.m., maybe you end up meeting this new client there. Now, if you were to go grocery shopping at 9 a.m., maybe you would end up meeting your next collaborator. Life is that magical, and every choice creates a new path. It is up to us to select which path we would like to take.

That being said, I do believe the universe plays a huge role in our decision-making. For example, if someone has really bad intentions, I personally believe the universe will step in and try to stop you from meeting, or working with, or connecting with that person. Have you also ever noticed that when you try to force something, or push someone to do something, or try to manipulate a situation to get your way, it usually backfires? We do have free will, but I also believe there is divine timing for everything. I believe we can't really force things or we will receive a ton of pushback. But the most incredible thing in life is that for every path we take that costs us a "mistake," we also receive a lesson from it. And so there is no real such thing as failure, only a way to realize what you want and do not want.

Like when I tried rushing to get my TV show pilot edited and I ended up going through three different editors to do it. This was not only because I had very little patience, but also because I was not more selective of what I wanted. I was in a desperate state of mind to just have anyone and everyone who has access to the editor edit it. I should have, from the beginning, really sat down with myself and got a clear picture of what I wanted and then hired that person, versus hiring just anyone for timing's sake just to get it done. Doing something just to get it done is the wrong approach and will set you up for failure.

Even after I finally found the right editor, I had to bring in two more other editors just to mentor that editor. In total, I had five editors throughout the project from start to finish. Did I regret it? No, because in life there are always learning lessons. But my point is, why rush something? Why not take your time? Why not make something epic versus good? This is a hard lesson I had to realize: the lesson of patience, taking my time, having faith, and creating space for things to flow and not forcing things to work.

So if you choose to start looking at life like a game, it will become one giant adventure. You see, it is not so much about the destination but the journey, obstacles, characters, and learning lessons that make life such a fascinating venture! Now, along with being in the game of life comes the magic of being in the right place at the right time. Now you might ask yourself, how does one get to this place? After all, life is not just about strategy but also about energy. And so if you ask me, how does one get to a place of bringing so many amazing people, opportunities, and pure magic into their life? My answer would be, "Well, my friend, being in alignment is the key."

When it comes to our mistakes, we can always learn from them. No one said being in business was easy. No one said having a brand was easy. No one said making money was easy. No one said finding the ideal clients was a perfect process. Sometimes you will have clients who are not the best fit. Sometimes you will have clients who ask for a refund. Sometimes you will hear a no and it is all OKAY. That is the adventure of being in business. It is truly a wild ride.

The important thing is staying power. Staying with it. Staying consistent. Keeping at it. No matter what challenges arise. You stay. You continue. You fall and get yourself up. And you keep going. As a leader in business, I am here to help guide you.

Remember that life and business is not about perfection, okay? It is about consistency. It is about the willpower to keep going even when it gets tough. Remember your why and why you decided to do this in the first place. When it comes down to looking deep within, it is not usually about money, it is about something bigger. That's your why. If you are reading this book, the odds are it is about making an impact in some way. The people I attract into my world have big visions and dreams for themselves and the world.

As a coach and consultant, I hold space for people to empower themselves. The coach is not the power, they are the tool you can utilize to help you realize your own potential. I have been teaching my clients how to shift their own energetic field so they can attract more of the things they want in their life. One of my clients texted me that someone offered to pay for his groceries. This was so exciting to hear. All I do is help people learn how to take their power back and how to tap into their own resources. He also told me that he started getting big commissions in his workplace ever since he hired me as his coach. It is truly so amazing how powerful you are, and when you tap into that, what you can do is unlimited. I really enjoy helping people take their businesses and brands to the next level.

Emotions and Frequency

This is a reminder that you are more capable than you think. This is a reminder to also never give up on your dreams. Lastly, I want to invite you to view every challenge as an opportunity to learn and grow. Look at life like one giant video game. There are always more ways to level up. People may challenge you but you will grow from these experiences.

If someone tends to trigger you emotionally, really take a hard look and ask yourself, "Why is this bothering me?" Is it reflecting something you do not like about yourself? Is it something that happened from your past that is evoking this feeling at the present moment? Really pay attention. Having self-awareness is crucial. When you get caught up in your emotions, you can block your own success. Therefore, working on managing your emotions and not letting them control you and your life is a big key to your success.

Affirmations

- My biggest mistakes are my greatest blessings.

- There is no such thing as the wrong path, just a different one.

- No matter what path I choose, I will always end up at the right place eventually.

- My mistakes are just lessons in disguise.

- My challenges are my biggest opportunities and doorways.

Top Tips

1. If something doesn't work out, do not force it.

2. Know that every choice creates a new path and if you do not end up where you wanted, you can always choose a different path.

3. If you feel like you failed, you did not. You just learned a lesson. You can turn every mistake into a lesson.

4. View being an entrepreneur as a "choose your own adventure." Every mistake is part of the journey.

5. Be prepared for when things do not go your way and know that that is okay.

6. Consistency is key. Stay with it even when things get hard.

7. Focus on your why.

8. Remember your power.

Lessons Learned

- Staying power is key to success.

- Being in business helps train you for problem-solving and communication skills.

- When you shift your energy, everything else can shift.

This Chapter Is Sponsored By

Polychromatic Records
www.chroma.boutique

Chapter 3

Gratitude Changes the Game

Gratitude will bring you more of whatever you are grateful for. Start practicing gratitude even for just waking up. Do you know the biggest secret to success? The biggest secret is gratitude. This is something every successful person knows.

How can you start implementing more gratitude into your life today?

1. Have a gratitude journal. Write out a list of things you are grateful for.

2. Every time you get paid or you receive something awesome, celebrate!

3. Write out a list of things you are grateful for that have not happened yet, but put it in the past tense. In other words, create the future.

Examples:

"I am so grateful for winning that Grammy last year!"

"I am so happy I found my dream manager, they're everything I could have ever asked for!"

4. Tell someone how much you appreciate having them in your life.

5. Every day, say thank you for waking up and being alive! Notice all the small but amazing things in your life. From the bed you sleep in, to the clothes you have, the electricity in your place, the guitar you play, etc.

Bonus tip!

Write a letter to yourself and thank yourself for being there for you and how much you love and appreciate yourself. Your relationship with receiving anything in your life is directly related to how much you love yourself. So be so kind to yourself!

Gratitude and The Heart Space

We are moving from the 3D, which is more about ego, to the 5D which is about heart-centered reality. Which means that anything you do, if it doesn't align with your heart and what you truly want, it will not work out. In order to receive more of what you do want, it is so important to be grateful. When you are in the frequency of gratitude, you are tapping into your heart space. Gratitude is the key to receiving more of what you desire. Also, the better you feel, the more you will attract things at a higher level vibration. So if you are grateful for a job and keep thanking God, or the universe, or your guides, or whatever you believe in for that opportunity, having that gratitude will help you attract even more opportunities.

It is also important to be grateful for your friendships, business, clients, and anything else you can think of. The amount of gratitude you show others will also be returned to you. You receive what you put out. Always remember that! Make sure to show gratitude and appreciation for everyone and everything in your life, even the learning lessons. Having gratitude will bring you to the next level in your life. Maybe that annoying boss was meant to teach you how to stand up for yourself. Maybe that friendship was not meant to last forever.

I also strongly believe that if something is aligned for you, it will work out. Having gratitude puts you on the highest frequency and therefore, will attract people and opportunities at the highest level as well. When you step into that frequency of appreciation and gratitude, it will also help detract people who are not for you anymore. You will notice some relationships might fade into the abyss and new ones could pop up fast. When you are in a state of gratitude, it helps you align with joy and encourages you to follow your passion and purpose more too! When you are happier, you will be more motivated to achieve things. So incorporate gratitude into your life and do things that make your heart sing as often as possible!

Manifesting

Speaking of gratitude, one of the biggest things I teach my clients is how to start being grateful for the money they receive so they can attract even more of it. A client shared with me that he had made more money ever since our call. One of my clients/friends had told me a similar thing. Since I taught her about the energetics of money and being grateful, she had also received a ton of opportunities and money.

Listen to Your Heart, Trust Your Gut, Tune Out Others

It is so important to listen to your heart when it comes to making decisions, and be grateful for those decisions. Trust your body, trust your heart, trust your soul, but do not trust your mind. Your mind will drive you absolutely crazy sometimes! You can go from indecision to indecision. If something does not work out, do not stress about it. Know that if it is meant to happen, it will! Then learn to just trust your body and be grateful to your body for always leading you. Speak to your body as if it is a person. Tell your body how grateful you are for it. Take care of your body so you can really be attuned with it and be able to tap into your intuition as much as possible.

Meditating is one way to start being more in tune with your body. When you meditate, show gratitude, and say how grateful you are to the universe, or God, or your angels for bringing all the people and amazing opportunities into your life. Do not focus on just the mind. Listening to your mind can only leave you feeling trapped. The key is to listen to your body. Does your body feel expanded or contracted when making decisions? Does speaking to that person give you anxiety or make you feel calm? Pay attention to how your body feels when it comes to making every decision. Also, if you feel fear, ask yourself, "Is it because my ego is getting in my way, or is it truly not good for me?"

No matter what others tell us, it is most important to listen to ourselves first. At the end of the day, only we know in our heart what is best for us. We have to tune out the noise of the opinions of others and ultimately, follow the path we see fit that makes us happy. The happier we are, the more successful we will become. We will also never ever be able to please everyone. So why bother living your life to make everyone else happy or make them "approve" you? Do you really need to hear a "good job" for self-validation? We can validate ourselves. We can feel proud of ourselves. We can learn to love ourselves more.

When it comes to gratitude, it is also very essential to celebrate our wins! When we celebrate what is going well in our life, we become a magnet for more and more of it. So celebrating your wins is a huge key to bringing in more of what you want into your life. I always advise my clients to have a notebook where they track their wins daily! Even tracking your wins weekly is a great start. It could be as simple as: I got out of bed today, or I just did laundry, or I just made myself food, or I made time to meditate. It can also be as big as: I just got my dream job, or I am moving into my dream home, or I just found the love of my life.

Grab a notebook and start writing your wins every single day! You can even add fun stickers or write them in colored markers if you want. Make it a beautiful and fun experience. A daily habit, if you will. When our brain can find positive things to be grateful for, it will start looking for more positive things and find more evidence of why things are going well in your life.

Business Wins

Here are some business wins that I am so incredibly grateful for!

- Helped my client connect with a producer and she recorded a song for the first time.

- Got one of my clients an opportunity to co-write with me for a film.

- Created a pilot episode for my TV show!

- Released my singles "Unapologetic" and "Gone."

- Threw a release party for "Unapologetic" and did a live performance and showcase event.

- Filmed my first professional music video for my single "Unapologetic."

Top Tips

I was meditating on the audio frequency 420 Hz which is all about healing. When I got up, I got inspired to make reels or jewels of wisdom. I felt called to share. So the following are some of those jewels. I feel like these messages were practically channeled. Apply them to your life as you see fit. Whatever you resonate with is great, whatever you do not, that's fine too!

1. The more you worry about something, the more you build momentum for it to happen. So the key is to step back, breathe, and go back to where you find your peace.

2. As an artist, you have magic within you from your lyrics and music. Did you know music is all about vibrations? So every time you're making music, you're impacting people's lives, their subconscious, and their moods. Did you know you have the power to make beautiful, incredible, powerful music that can change people's lives? The world needs your voice. Your voice is like magic.

3. Daily affirmations to say to yourself in the mirror every day: "I love you so much. You are so powerful. You are so beautiful. You are so incredible. You are capable of so much more than you even know. You have so much magic inside of you. You can literally do anything and I am so excited for you to see all the magic you are going to create in your life!"

4. Also be thankful for the things that trigger you and make you angry because it is actually showing you what you need to heal within yourself. So instead of being really pissed off at someone and saying, "You suck!" You can instead say, "Thank you for showing me that this is still in my subconscious as a trauma and is something I still need to heal. I am grateful for the opportunity to grow and become an even more up-level person."

5. Let's also talk about the stories we tell ourselves. We are basically in a movie all the time. Our lives are being played out by the stories we tell ourselves. So what story are you telling yourself? Are you telling yourself you're happy and amazing, that your life is awesome, and you attract the most amazing shit ever? Or

are you telling yourself your life sucks, that things are awful, and things are stressful 24/7 and it just gets worse? Which story are you telling yourself? It is up to you. You're the main character. Choose the story that you want. ;)

6. Also, when did we decide that we have to be perfect and happy 24/7? Can we just start playing this game called loving ourselves more, stepping into our power more, and just play around with that vibe? We have so much self-hate and are so hard on ourselves, and yet expect ourselves to be perfect 24/7. Well, guess what? We are not perfect. We will never be perfect. We are human, divine, and magical. And we can still choose to love ourselves.

7. Raise your vibration. You gotta do things that make you happy. Take walks, listen to music that you love, talk to people that make you feel good on the phone, perform on live streams, see your friends, order food, make cookies. Whatever it is, do something that will make you happy.

8. It is also funny that we get so mad at each other for having different beliefs, perspectives, etc. But that's what makes the world a beautiful place. That is what makes humanity so incredible. How bored would we be if everyone just agreed with what we said and did what we said? It would be like, "What's the point?" Right? So it is all about growing and understanding each other, and of course, love.

9. The ironic part is that, the minute we stop caring and we surrender, when we don't take it so seriously and become less harsh on ourselves, that is when we actually take back our power to be happy because we aren't giving other people our

power to make us happy. And that's like freedom.

10. It is funny how we spend so much time and energy making other people happy instead of actually just doing what makes us happy and making that the important thing. We live our lives for other people and it means so much when other people approve of us or give us validation.

Power of Peace

A wise friend once gave me great advice: Go to your peace. In other words, go to what makes you feel at peace. As an empath, it's really easy for me to get energetically overwhelmed especially when I spend too much focus across social media. But this is my new mantra: Go to where your peace is at. This is my new focus. The more at peace we are, the more in alignment we become. The more in alignment we become, the more we attract the right opportunities, etc.

So the key to getting more of what you want and achieving overall happiness? It's simply to feel better. Your job is to get into alignment. Of course, if you have a core belief that you will only get things if you push and work really, really hard, then that will be your reality. But, what if you opened up your mind to the possibility that by feeling good, you actually become in alignment with everything you want? And it becomes easier and easier, the better you feel. It's quite interesting how much mental energy we put on what we do not want to happen, and then wonder why it happened.

The truth is, the more resistance you put on something, the more you attract it. The more you go with the flow and don't push against something with so much energy, the more at ease life will become for you. When we try, and try, and try, and work hard but are working from the scarcity mindset, we will create much resistance. If we focus on good-feeling thoughts and what feels light, we will have a much easier time attracting those things we really, really want.

So my challenge for you is to really focus on one to three things you can do every day to feel good. Another challenge is to pay attention to every text you receive, every email, every avenue of communication, your everyday language, the words you speak about your life and yourself and others, and see them as reflections of what you're choosing to focus on. Be intentional with the people you listen to and spend your time with because every single person you're around will either bring you up or down. They will affect your energy. So like I said in the beginning, go to where your peace is at. I invite you to let go of what no longer serves you.

Things Happen for a Reason

Keep in mind that the universe always has your back. If you have a client who is awful to work with and they find an excuse to ask for a refund, let them go. If you have a friend who is toxic, drives you insane, and gets in a fight with you, let them go. If you hired someone but it is not working out, let them go. The universe has our back and will shift things to make room for bigger, better, and greater things that are more in alignment with us.

So the next time you get ready to curse out the world because something didn't work out, remember it's just the way the universe makes room for bigger and better things for you. :) Learn to let things go and make room for the new! And remember to pay close attention to how people make you feel, that is the key! If it stresses you out to be around them or talk to them, let them go, fire them, move on! If they make you feel inspired or expanded, you know that is a good person to have in your corner!

Heart Versus Mind: Raising Your Vibration

If you are feeling down or in a bad mood, try dancing! When we move our bodies, we raise our vibration. In other words, we will start to feel better. We shift the energy. So create movement and watch magic happen. Other ways are resting, taking a walk, meditating, and so on. But moving our bodies is a big key for creating shifts. The more shifts we can create, the more we can move the energy from being stagnant to flowing to overflowing! It is the simple changes, rituals, or habits we bring into our life that can make all the impact. Listen to your body. What is it saying? Is it saying it's tired? Then rest. If it is overactive, then try walking. If it is saying, "Go call that person to ask about that opportunity," then do it. But let your body lead, not your mind.

We can get stuck in our mind over, and over, and over, and over. Our thoughts can repeat a multitude of times. The same thoughts, the same old stories, and the same old beliefs. If you want to shift this, start to create new habits in your life. Move some things around. Try a new place to eat. Try a new path to walk somewhere. Switch things up. Get rid of old things in your room, reorganize things, give away clothes you no longer want. Buy a new instrument. Spend less energy with people who bring you down and spend more energy with people who hold space for you to be the best version of yourself.

Find love within yourself. Find happiness and peace within yourself. Follow your bliss. Do what makes you happy and the money will follow. Start feeling with your body versus chasing with your mind. It will make all the difference. You start to see that life is a journey, not a race. It is not about the finish line, it is not about getting an X amount of Grammys. Life is an adventure! Life is about experiencing all of it. Life is about the magic in the small things! Appreciate the small things and more magic will come into your life. Hold gratitude just for waking up today. Hold gratitude for the friendships in your life.

Start a gratitude journal. Write down a few things every day that you're grateful for. Start a possibility journal where you write out ten things that would be fun if it happened! It all starts with the small things, small shifts. What small things can you start incorporating into your life to create shifts?

Detoxing from Social Media

I just tried something. I removed the Instagram (IG) app from my phone as an experiment and I have noticed the following:

- Easier time to focus and zone in on tasks

- Better peace of mind

- Less stress

- Happier

- Able to sit still for longer periods of time

I noticed that not looking at my IG 24/7 and comparing myself to everyone, and not having to worry about people liking my posts was really helping my mental health. A lot of times when I post on IG, I feel this pressure of needing to get X amount of likes. And when a person does not like my post, I question why and start thinking, "Wow, my content must not be as valuable because only Y amount of people liked X post." But that is not true. First of all, IG hides most of our posts unless you are following and engaging with that person often or paying for ads. So most people that are following you are not even seeing your content so do not be so hard on yourself.

I have noticed that not being on IG gave me more time to focus on specific tasks. It was such an addiction before that I checked my app every five minutes. Now, I actually have time to get things done, or meditate, or have space for myself to think or visualize. It is also not about being busy 24/7 either, it is about creating space and pockets of time to get things done and pockets of time to rest. Especially if you work at home and are an entrepreneur, it's easy to want to work 24/7 or never get any work done due to being on IG. I am not hating on IG; I love reels, etc. but I am just challenging you to take a break for a month and see what happens and how you feel.

Lessons Learned

1. The happier you are, the more you will attract what you want into your life.

2. People who challenge you will only help you become a stronger entrepreneur or business person.

3. The more you can identify your triggers, the stronger you will become.

4. The more you listen to your heart and body, the better your body knows before your mind.

5. Learn to embrace people's perspectives that are different from your own.

6. The more you focus on your peace of mind, the more abundance you will attract.

7. The more you focus on needing something, the more you push it away.

8. When you feel emotional, try moving your body—dancing, walking, running, etc. Moving your body is key to releasing emotions and then you will feel so much better.

9. The more you give yourself a break from social media, the more you can focus. Be really aware of how much time you spend on it.

Affirmations

- I am so grateful for all the blessings that come into my life daily.

- I'm so grateful that the right people and opportunities always show up.

- I'm so grateful to have peace of mind every single day.

- I'm so grateful for all the abundance that comes into my life every day.

- I'm so grateful for all the beauty, wonder, and joy that come into my life every day.

- I'm so grateful for all the incredible creativity and ideas that come to me every single day.

- I'm so grateful for all the amazing people that show up in my life. My soulmate clients, my soulmate collaborators, and anyone else that is in alignment for my highest good and purpose.

This Chapter Is Sponsored By

Brei Carter
www.breicarter.com

Chapter 4

Trust The Damn Process

Synchronicity

Dear Diary,

I am so excited! I should be receiving the next cut for our show. I am in PA for my sister's wedding. I got my hair cut by my family's client's place and one of the haircutters happens to be in a rock band LOL. And his brother happens to work in film in NY. He even told me that someone he knew is married to the president of Columbia Records. They were supposed to show them his music a while ago. He told me to send him the pilot once it is done and he will show it to his brother. He even watched my intro and smiled! I could see my show inspired him and it felt so good!

One more win I will share with you is that I heard back from a guy who invested in a major musical called "Waitress." He read my script for our musical and he wants to hear demos next. So I am having my writer Zac, who we made the musical about his album years ago, come up with different parts. And then I will need a few singers to demo the songs.

xoxo,
Dani

It is funny because so many things have happened at the exact same time I wrote this diary entry. It is like when you show up for something important, the universe is like, "Okay, cool. You are doing your thing. So while you are doing your thing, we are going to help you a hundred times." Like literally, ten things in one day. I am like, "WOW, so grateful." It's like boom! Boom! Boom! Boom! Boom! Thank you, Universe! When you are not focused on something, you have less resistance to it and therefore, it comes in faster. Like when you are not focused on selling something, or making money, or getting something done because your mind is on other things, then magically, people come to you and are like, "Let me pay you!"

When in Doubt, Reach Out

I thought to myself, "Damn, I LOVE this song by this famous band in the UK called Nothing But Thieves. My friend introduced me to their music and I thought, "OMG! I desire to have their song in my TV show." They are signed to Sony but I thought of emailing their management just for fun. When I researched their management, I found out that the owners of the management company also used to work with developing bands including New Found Glory, Something Corporate (Andrew McMahon), Steel Train (Jack Antonoff), Dashboard Confessional, The Starting Line, Hellogoodbye, The Early November, Senses Fail, and Finch. So now, they will know my name even if I get rejected.

But then again, why would they say no? If anything, they will just take a while to get back to me or say they need to see the pilot first, etc. Maybe even one of them could be a judge. Like who knows, right? No matter how big someone is, you won't know until you try to reach out.

So I casually asked them how much it would cost to license one of their songs in my TV show. I explained to them we are not sure yet which platform it will be on or who will be producing it but that I was just curious non-exclusively how much. I also offered to show them the pilot when it's done and told them it's a music competition show. I share this to encourage you to reach BIG, reach HIGHER. Reach out to that manager you always wanted to work with or that artist you love that you want to collaborate with or feature. Like, why not? You have nothing to lose unless you do not try, then you will never know. So my challenge for you is to think of someone you want to work with and go reach out to them!

Get Creative with Promotion

Get creative on ways to get attention on social media for your music. For example, when I got my haircut, I decided to turn it into a social media campaign. I created a reel showing a "before and after" then I synced my song "Unapologetic" in the reel so I could cross promote my name. Then I tagged my writers and the hair salon. Therefore, it was a win-win. You do not pay money out of pocket to sync music to content in Reels, so why not take advantage of that and use your own songs to sync to content you create?

Detachment

If you hold on to something and try to control the outcome, then you create resistance around it, making it harder to manifest. This is probably most important, detach from the outcome. Ask and then detach. So you gotta say, "Okay, I want X but I do not care if X comes into my life either way," and just go about your life! If you feel like "OMG, I need this to happen or I will not be happy," then you are in the LACK vibration, not the ABUNDANCE vibration. Big difference.

Letting Go of Control

At the end of the day, the only thing we have control over is what we choose to focus our energy, time, mindset, thoughts, stories, and beliefs on. The rest is out of our control. Spiraling in anxiety about *anything* we have no control over is a waste of our energy. You really want to make an impact? Focus on peace, love, and good energy. Stay in a high vibration and see where you can create peace within yourself and your own friends and family. The best thing you can do if you want to make an impact is stay in a high vibration. Listen to music that helps uplift you. Write music, channel any emotions into creative projects.

Your mind is like a magnet. The thoughts you choose to think about magnetize what you see. So whatever is it you want to see happen, visualize that. It is also safe to feel. There is no wrong emotion. We are human and will never be perfect. It is safe to cry, scream, get mad, but try not to stay in that emotion as the everyday vibe. Feel it, then move on to something you do have control over.

I also like the Serenity Prayer by Reinhold Niebuhr:

"God grant me the serenity to accept the things I cannot change, courage to change the things I can, and the wisdom to know the difference. Living one day at a time; enjoying one moment at a time; accepting hardships as the pathway to peace. Taking as He did the sinful world as it is, not as I would have it. Trusting that He will make all things right if I surrender to His will. That I may be reasonably happy in this world and supremely happy with Him forever in the next. Amen."

Things Happen for a Reason

Remember, life is all about intention. What intentions do you want to set out? How intentional are you in your own life? Everything from what food you choose to eat, who you spend your time with, who you hire on your team to serve your music or business, to the words you say daily, words you write daily, conversations you have, what messages you listen to, and the messages in the music you listen to, and beyond. The more intentional you become in your life, the more power you have in your life, and the more life will start to be a fun adventure!

Alignment

So what does being in alignment actually mean? When we think of life as a game, we can think of being in alignment as having cheat codes for the game. It will make it way easier and a smoother process. We can either go with the flow or we can create resistance and push against the universe. Because we have free will, we have the freedom to make choices even if they are not in alignment with us. And one way or the other, we will learn lessons from our choices. But when you are ready to get into alignment, that is when you start seeing some magical results.

Have you ever looked at someone and asked, "Damn, why is that artist having so much more success than me, or how is that author taking off, or why did that video go viral on TikTok?" How did they do that? Part of the answer to that is because they were in alignment. So what is alignment exactly? When I define alignment, I basically mean that you are bringing into your life the right people, money, opportunities, and so on that are a vibrational energetic match to your energy. I am sure you are wondering, "In English please, Dani?"

Okay, so basically, this means you attract people into your life that are a match to you energetically. Think of this like matching keys and locks. If you are in a low vibrational energetic state of mind, you will attract people that probably are angry, selfish, rude, disrespectful, complaining, really sad, etc. If you are in a high energetic state of mind, you will attract people that are happy, giving, supportive, and so on. :) This will be the same for every opportunity, collaborator, work circumstance, etc. So my point is, if you want to speed up your success, start consciously every day, by stepping more and more into better-feeling emotions.

The happier you are, the more you will attract happy people and opportunities that match that. Start thinking about what kind of people you surround yourself with are in alignment with you and what you want in life. If you find yourself constantly around many people in low emotional states, chances are you will find yourself being in the same. We are who we surround ourselves with so really think about who you want in your inner circle in all aspects of your life.

Power of Intentions

The power of intention and the people you choose to work with are key to your success. If clients feel draining to work with or are not paying you what you want, you will not have a powerful intention to want to help them. Therefore, you will not have the powerful results you desire for them. Choose the people to work with who make you feel good!

Set intentions and make sure you are intentional with the clients you choose to take on. Make sure you're getting paid what feels good to you. Otherwise, you will take it out on your client or not put in the effort you want.

No matter what business, as an artist or an entrepreneur, it all comes down to:

1. Figuring out your offer

2. Figuring out your price

3. Figuring out your target market

4. Figuring out your content strategy to reach those clients

5. Setting up systems in place to capture leads and build that container

6. Learning how to sell

7. Mindset

Honestly, mindset is 90% of sales, success, and everything but the rest are also important. ;) So anyway, long story short, these are what I help people with:

- Building their brand

- Figuring out their audience

- Being more intentional in their business or brand

- Identifying anything in their own way belief-wise

- Helping them step into the next level version of themselves

There is something so powerful that happens when people step into my world. Here are some examples:

- One of our clients went from thinking she wanted to sell only physical products to realizing her true desire is creating a whole healing space to sell her products.

- One of our clients went from being afraid to be on camera to doing her first interview and being excited to share her message to the world.

- One of our clients got asked to be featured on a podcast with hundreds of thousands of followers.

- One of our clients that consulted our team on content strategy over two years ago has grown his TikTok to five hundred thousand followers within only a couple of years.

- One of our clients, within one call, went from being afraid to perform to building out a set to perform monthly.

- One of our clients went from just having ideas of what products to sell to launching her own online store.

Your intention behind everything is everything. Ask yourself, what is the intention behind everything you do in your life? For example, if you do not want to do something but you still do it out of guilt, the intention behind it is weak. That means, you will not have successful results as you would if it was something you actually wanted to do.

Stand strong in your intentions. Do what you truly feel called to do. Whether that is the people you choose to be around, the people you date, the mentors you hire, the team you hire, or the people you collaborate with, make sure you feel good about being around them. Make sure you feel good about the music you are putting out. When you have a strong intention, you will create a better outcome for that project or person you have the intention to be around.

It is the energy behind the things you put effort into that will make the difference. If you feel like you need to post on social media but you are thinking, "I do not want to post right now. I am tired," then that post will not reach as many people. Everything comes down to energy and intention. Remember to be intentional with everything you do.

Top Tips

1. Always put yourself out there and take the chance because you never know. If you do not ever take the risk, you 100% can't win the opportunity.

2. Show up for important things and stop trying to focus so much on an area where you are lacking. The universe will make space to bring you what you want.

3. Detach from the outcome. To receive what you want faster, you must surrender.

4. Focus on what you have control over which are your reactions, thoughts, beliefs, etc. and let go of the rest.

5. The more we feel, the more we heal! This is something my friend Jourdan Rystrom says all the time to me!

6. When things do not work the way we planned, know that the universe has a better and bigger plan for us!

7. Try to stay in alignment as often as possible to attract what you desire in your life.

8. Make sure to set powerful intentions. Your intentions are everything. This means, choose clients that you feel good around, choose pricing you are happy with, and choose the intentions you want people to have when working with you.

Affirmations

- I give it up to God, or the universe, or my angels.

- Things are always happening for me in the perfect divine timing.

- God's timing over when I want it to happen.

- I attract the perfect people at the perfect time for whatever it is I'm looking to do.

- I surrender it to the universe.

- My intentions will lead the way.

- Energy first, aligned action second.

- My energy and alignment will always guide me.

- When I let go, I receive.

- Divine timing always.

This Chapter Is Sponsored By

Tim Shepherd
www.tscoproperties.com

Chapter 5

Know Your Worth (Then Add Interest)

Have you ever had a client who makes you feel drained, tired, stressed, or anxious? That is a sign. If you feel this in your body, RUN. Sometimes, we think, "Oh, we are receiving money. Great!" But sometimes, the client is not worth the stress. There are other clients out there that are better suited for you. You never have to settle. Please never settle.

I attracted a client into my life who wanted me to do a music video for really low. First, I was like, "Great, let's do it." Then I realized I do not usually do videos so putting together a whole video team was really stressing me out. Second, his budget and expectations did not line up. It was not worth the headache and the pressure.

Ironically, clients that want to do everything super cheap also end up being the most nit-picky. They end up trying to take the most of your time. I felt this feeling in my gut like, "Dani, ask for more $." So I asked for an additional payment of about $900. What was their response? "No." Could I have reacted and said, "Omg, why not?" Beg for money? Try to explain the value, etc.? Maybe, but that would be so pointless. Not every client is for us. Please always remember your worth. It is not worth settling. Not everyone—songwriter, singer, instrumentalist, producer, marketing team, or even coach—will be an ideal match for you. When we let go of one person in our life, we make room for someone new. When we let go of clients that do not align with us, we make space for new ones.

Do you ever ponder on your standards? I had the pleasure of sitting down at the Penthouse of Mastro's Steakhouse in Beverly Hills. I had to do some last-minute shopping thirty minutes before the meeting because I did not own the appropriate clothes to make the right impression for the casual dinner meeting I was about to have. As we drove through Beverly Hills, it hit me how I had forgotten that I have the right to have standards. I was reminded that I do not have to settle. Sitting down with a multimillionaire who travels 24/7 really inspired me of what is really possible.

Sometimes we forget. Sometimes, we do not travel or move; we just stay still and get caught up in our head, spinning the same thoughts over, and over, and over. When we travel and get out of our comfort zone, this is where we really find a new set of standards, new possibilities, and a new level that's ten times higher.

I also had a realization and was reminded of how the people we surround ourselves with makes all the difference in the world—in our mindset, our income, our relationships, and in what is possible. Do you ever ask yourself, how can I bring more into my life? How can I find the people that do what I want to do to make my dreams come true? How can I work with that dream producer, artist, songwriter? How can I get my TV show off the ground? Who do I need to talk to, to make it possible? What manager do I need to work with to help support my music career? What festival bookers do I need to connect with to really get booked? How can I do better? How can I work less but make more impact, achieve more transitions, and level up?

Let me tell you, it is about knowing the right people and having the right relationships. One person can make an impact. One person can really change your life for the better. So it is not so much about collecting a million business cards. It is about figuring out the path you want to go and teaming up with people who can help you get there. It is about alignment. So my point is, stop settling and start aligning with the right people. Be purposeful and intentional and you will go so far, farther than you could have ever imagined.

Story Time!

I got an opportunity. Fifty songs got selected to be pitched for a pre-cleared catalog for a commercial. Fifty! And I had about four days to get clearance from each artist. Talk about pressure! One by one, I contacted every artist via text, email, or both. Some of these artists I have not spoken to in months!

When it comes to sync, meeting the deadlines are everything. Plus, our time is valuable so I do not have four days to spend just contacting artists. I then decided that I had to do it in the next twenty-four to forty-eight hours. Whoever is in, great! Whoever disapproves, no big deal! My mission either way was simple: to get an answer, yes or no.

As I approached each artist, and explained to them the budget and terms, etc., everyone was thrilled! I thought, "Wow, this is easy!" Then there was one artist who said "maybe" and that they will get back to me in my timeline. I thought to myself, "Maybe?! My time is valuable. Come on, silly woman, let's go!" I texted her and she said she will try to get back to me. But I wanted to send the answers that day, so I told her to let me know by the end of the day or I just will not approve any of her songs for this potential opportunity. I could not legally approve without the artist/songwriter's consent. I told myself, "Wow, this girl is not ALL-IN." She does not respect my time or energy to help her get this opportunity.

This kind of behavior did not align with me, it is either you are ALL-IN or you're OUT. I did not have time to waste waiting on one artist when everyone else was able to totally make the deadline. I said to myself, "I think I want to drop her from the catalog. This is a waste of time and energy." If someone does not respect my time or energy, for me, it is not worth it. Sorry, not sorry. I invite all of you to have a similar mindset. Your time is valuable! If someone does not respect your time, they are not worth your time. You are valuable and priceless. Your health, stress levels, and mindset are everything. If you have a client who stresses you out for any reason, and is causing more stress than good, let them go.

Anyway, this whole time, my stomach was hurting, so I was not in the best mood. But I knew I needed to get this done because all these artists were relying on me. So I had to push through it. I decided to follow up with her one more time the next day. I told the company that I was waiting on one artist out of the fifty songs. So I expected a yes or no the next day but instead, what I got was an email from her asking to be dropped from our contract. Wow, my mindset manifested this LOL. I was thinking I should drop her as she was not aligned. Then boom! She says to me let's end our contract. The universe was clearly dropping out the people who do not align with me. Has something like this ever happened to you?

Top Tips

1. Set high standards for yourself and your business. Do not just take on ANYONE as a client out of desperation. Really be intentional with who you choose to work with.

2. If someone does not respect you or your time, they are not worth your time. Let them go.

3. If you are ever interested in sync, make sure you meet the deadlines. If you have questions, that's fine. But if someone

gives you all the info that's provided, please make it easy on the person as they are spending time. They are not getting paid upfront to help you so just respect their time. Simple. :)

4. Especially if you do anything for free, make sure it is aligned with you.

5. I do not advocate working for free. Usually, people you work for for free respect you the least LOL.

6. If you are committed, go ALL-IN, not half way. Do whatever it takes.

7. My standard for my clients is ALL-IN. You are either in or out; that's it! No in-between.

At the end of the day, the only person that has your back the most, is yourself. So why have such high expectations of others? Let's drop expectations and just focus more on self-love. We are all human, none of us are perfect. So why do we expect so much out of each other? Self-respect and self-love is a powerful thing. If anyone ever speaks down to you, please do not spend energy or time speaking to them.

Stepping Into Your Next Level

Dear Diary,

I know, it is like 3 a.m. as I type this but OH MY GOSH, so much has happened over the past month and I am trying to put it into words of wisdom to teach you so you can start applying it in your life.

*It all started a month ago. I told myself, "Dani, you are done playing small! It is time to step up into your NEXT LEVEL VERSION of Dani Felt... **Dani Felt 10.0**. Yes, not 2.0... 10.0. The Million Dollar Coach version of Dani Felt."*

I decided to start making decisions and think like the 10.0 version of myself. What would Dani 10.0 dress like? How would Dani 10.0 answer calls? How would Dani 10.0 answer emails? What would Dani 10.0 charge? What services would Dani 10.0 sell?

xoxo,
Dani

-oOo-

When you make decisions from this place, something really amazing happens, your whole world starts to reflect this. I know I have emphasized many times: What you think, you bring into your life. But it is also about who you are BEING, thinking like, acting like, speaking like that attracts the things and people in your life.

Boundaries

So what did I start doing that was different? I started setting higher standards for myself, my clients and my business. I made a firm decision: This is what I am okay with and this is what I am not okay with. Anytime something would come up that a client did or didn't do, I would bring it up or take action. For example, sometimes I post on Facebook and people like to promote their work in my comments, I immediately remove those comments.

I realized how much time I focused on finding talent. I spent hours of my week to find one singer for one project, for maybe $100. I'm over that waste of time. It was draining and felt tiring. When something feels tiring, your body is not aligned with it. If you are not aligned with it, you will find it harder to do the thing! The more things that feel aligned with you, feel good in your body, and you feel excited to do, the more power and success you will have doing those things. That is why doing things that bring you joy will bring you so much success.

At the same time, if you are relying only on that thing but are not bringing in money from it, then you are approaching it from a level of scarcity and it will be more difficult for you to sell that thing you're passionate about. So in that case, getting a side gig can really help you. Because when you approach people from a place of abundance and more than enough, then you will find it easier to sell. I digress, back to my main point.

So establishing boundaries was one of the first changes I made. Second was figuring out the amount that I wanted to charge for my services and my team's services. This has to feel good to both you and your clients. If you want to sell a t-shirt for your music for $1,000 but you don't feel worthy of receiving that, then it will be nearly impossible to find clients who would want to pay you that. So it all comes down to what feels good for you and your clients, both.

Third, I started getting super clear about my offers and what I choose to focus on selling, PR and Consulting, that is it. Fourth, I started getting clear on the type of clients and niches I wanted to work with. Honestly, at this point, I am very open but I have spoken to fashion labels, wellness coaches, artists, and comedians, and I realized the amount I offer can help so many different people. This helped shift my perspective to abundance. Thus, there is an abundant amount of clients.

If you are a producer. It is similar. There are millions of artists in the world, you only need a select few to be successful, depending on your rates of course. But say, you are charging $1500 per track as a producer and your goal is to make $10,000 per month. Well then, you need to close around six clients per month to achieve that. Only six out of millions of artists, it is 100% possible. Now, how fast you become successful will depend hugely on what you BELIEVE you are capable of. Your story is EVERYTHING. Once I realized all the different people I can help, I started shifting my story. I said to myself, "Of course, people will pay X price for X service. It is a no-brainer!" This shifted my perspective to there are millions of potential people who can purchase my services and products easily, now I just need to find a few.

Set boundaries from the start. If you do not set boundaries, do not expect people to necessarily give you what you want. Generally speaking, people are not mind readers so it is important to set clear rules so you can create space for yourself to succeed.

Lessons Learned

1. It is important to make a list of what you will and will not tolerate in your business. Create new rules and stick to them.

2. It is important to make a list of the type of clients you desire to work with. Design your client avatar.

3. It is important to write the story that you want to start choosing to believe and write in detail. You could start with journaling a day in the life of your next level self.

Self-worth Affirmations

- I am worthy of everything I desire.

- Massive success is the next step in my life.

- Being successful is happening more every day!

- I am worthy of so many incredible things happening in my life.

Know Your Worth

I was doing such intense Emotional Freedom Technique (EFT) with myself when I had a major self-discovery. For those of you who do not know what EFT is, it's a stress reduction technique that will help you unblock subconscious limiting beliefs and get to the root of what is triggering you emotionally. For example, if someone bothers you in line in the supermarket, it usually has nothing to do with THEM. Rather, it has something to do with YOU. When we get triggered, if we have emotions coming out of anxiety, fear, sadness, frustration, anger, or hopelessness, it usually reflects something within us, not the people triggering us.

I invite you to look deep within, why is this person triggering me? What is the root of this? It usually goes back to childhood, the stories you learned from past experiences, or thoughts our family or friends tell us. You are who you surround yourself with. So anyway, I was doing EFT and working out an issue on when people do not pay me, it bothers me so much and I always take it so personally. And then as I was tapping, I came to the conclusion that since I grew up learning to prioritize business and success, money and accomplishments, I realized that when people pay me I feel loved and so when people do not pay me, I feel like they do not love me. That is crazy and a limiting belief. Limiting beliefs are stories and beliefs in our subconscious mind that we think are true but are not.

As artists, we are business owners and I feel like sometimes we take things personally. If someone does not listen to our music, we take it personally like, OMG, I suck, or maybe my music is not good enough, maybe they do not care about me at all. I thought they are my friends, why aren't they streaming my song like a hundred times a day? They didn't share my new video, they must be upset with me, and the same thing with purchasing from you, etc., etc., etc. Know that, just because someone does not do something for you, it does not mean they do not love you or care about you.

Understand that everyone has their own lives, busy with their own things, and it is okay if they are prioritizing themselves over you. You are worthy for just being here, for being alive. Just because you have not won a Grammy yet does not mean you are not worthy. Just because you don't have one hundred thousand followers on Instagram does not mean you are not worthy. Everyone has their own journey and their own lessons and experiences. You are here for your own personal journey and experiences, so stop comparing yourself to others. And try not to take things so personally. I know that can be difficult but just try.

I invite you to think about the limiting beliefs you carry around that are not serving you. Time to sever ties with them and replace them with new stories. :)

Being Happy Is Not Selfish

Just because you want to be happy or put yourself first does not make you a bad person or selfish. When we fill our own cup, when we rise, we can help others better. It is okay to prioritize your wellbeing and happiness over everything else. Be selfish. Self-love is a powerful thing. If you do not want to do something, then DO NOT DO IT. If you are doing something just to make someone else happy, that is not good either. Do things you want to do. It is okay to be happy.

You are perfect just the way you are. Never try to change to be someone else to impress others. Be yourself and you will attract your right match at the right time. Things are always in alignment. You are always attracting people into your life that are a vibrational match to you. Remember, all the relationships in our lives are mirrors. Reflect on the people in your life and what lessons you learn from them. What do they teach you about yourself?

For those who are single and want to attract the right person, remember it starts with you. When you love yourself to the highest degree, you will attract people that treat you the same. Want to attract love? Start with self-love. Spoil yourself. Value yourself. Respect yourself. Do what makes you happy. Put yourself first. If you are feeling shame for being single or unworthy of love, just remember you are amazing just the way you are.

Keep shining your light. Keep showing love to yourself. Do what brings your heart joy and you will attract more joyful people. You are worthy of love. You are worthy of happiness. You are worthy of just being born. The world needs you and you make a difference in the world. Keep pursuing your dreams and the rest will follow.

Challenging Myself to Try New Things!

I decided to do an experiment called finding part-time work. I made it a game and told myself, "Okay, let's see what happens when you hyper focus." Within one week of applying, I got hired on the spot, but no interview was required. This should have been a red flag. But I thought, well, maybe I am meant to work there. Honestly, I am so used to working only for myself and being my own boss that I find this whole thing challenging—working for another aside from artists. I love working with artists.

This first part-time job was hostessing. Honestly, I was so naive and thought I would only be standing there and seating people or walking people to their seats. I soon realized this job is actually really challenging. You have to be really fast. You have to be able to problem-solve fast. You have to be able to communicate issues to staff. You have to be able to keep to the rules but also make others happy.

The first day, I said to myself, "Wow, I suck at this." It honestly shed light on all my weaknesses, but I told myself I would give it a month. A week later, I thought it would be fun to try playing the game of balance. I walked into another interview, at a place so close to where I lived and got hired on the spot again. This time, serving. Anyway, now I was in a position of playing the balancing act—two part-time jobs, working with my company, getting my TV show off the ground, and managing over twenty vendors along with other companies. How hard could it be? While still trying to memorize the seating chart for the first, I now had a second part-time job with an entire new seating chart and menu to memorize. I thought I could handle anything. Apparently, I thought I was superwoman and forgot I am human. Can someone please return my cape?

Anyway, it is so important for us to pay attention to our bodies and how we feel when we are around a certain situation. If we start to feel sadness, anger, frustration, or anxiety, it is a good idea to look at that and where it's being created from. Dreams are also a really good way to analyze our subconscious. Like when I had a nightmare about snakes all on my floor. Now, how do I feel about snakes? Absolutely terrified. I thought, why am I dreaming about this? You know, the day I started my job, the waiters joked with me about how long they think I will last there. That was my first red flag. I should have paid attention right there but thought, "Haha, they are being so funny," but really in the back of my mind I was like, hmmm…

The second red flag was the amount of pay they offered. I will not go into the details but it was way below what I felt my rate should be. Even though I took it happily and naively, I realized quickly that the pay was the way it is for a reason. After the first day of working, even though I was only a hostess, I also took it upon myself, I wrote out an entire list of marketing ideas for their business because that is what I do; I solve problems and offer solutions. It is what I am really good at, making money. And, no, they never asked me to do this. I just assumed, of course, that they would listen to me. My ego was proud. A few days later, I kept talking to the servers and realized no one seemed really happy there. I started getting flashback feelings of how I felt working with a past restaurant in NYC that also paid me way below my worth and caused me so much anxiety, I almost ended up with an ulcer.

You see, you slowly become who you surround yourself with. The third red flag was when they texted me casually on a Friday night, "Can you come in, I know it is last minute?" I had Friday nights off. They texted me two hours before my shift would have started. I said to myself that the universe is giving me an opportunity to bring in more abundance, and so I said, no problem. A day later, I realized that was a dumb move on my part as we teach people how to treat us. I said, "Damn it Dani, if you say yes, it means they will always try to take advantage."

A day later was the night of my event, and I specifically told them I had an event. But still they texted me again asking if I could come in. You know, that night, I felt so angry and triggered. I was angry with myself for saying yes when I should've said no. I had to set a boundary or I was going to yell. I calmly texted them, "Sorry, but I cannot come in. I am running an event and I cannot work on weekend nights. I just got a second part-time job." I finally set that boundary and felt better.

For the second part-time job, it said that I will work around five hours per shift. I said, "Okay, cool. I can handle that." So I left exactly five hours later and they looked at me like, why are you leaving early? I was clearly not supposed to take them literally. So I asked for clarification, "I remember you mentioning in the beginning that it would be X amount of hours. Am I wrong here? What are the exact hours?" They then went on to tell me that in the summertime, they actually expect me to work all the way until 11 p.m. or even midnight.

My body immediately felt resistance and was a hard NO to this. I said to myself, "This is not worth the really low pay." I am worthy of more. I can do better. This is not feeling good in my soul. I remember I started crying out of nowhere and I was asking myself what was wrong. I now realize, it was the energy I was around. You see, being an empath, I am sensitive to energy. Still some good came out of it. One of the hostesses who's a single mom started sharing with me her money issues and I shared with her about how to bring more money into her life and she thanked me. So at least I helped one person, that felt good.

But I knew, when I sent my management marketing ideas and he did not say anything within two weeks of working there, I knew I was not ever going to be appreciated for my marketing there. And let's face it, that was not in the job description. So I own up to that. I also knew the pay going in and decided to be upset about it later. I started crying and felt something was wrong. I watched myself get really angry and triggered and my heart started racing and I almost had an anxiety attack. I knew something was wrong and I had to pay attention. I felt in my gut, leave this place, this energy is not an aligned match for you. So I told them that I cannot be there anymore. That I took on too many things and my mental and physical health are more important to me.

My point is, know your worth. Do not settle. Listen to your body and look for the signs. I hope this story helps you in whatever way it is meant to. But also do not be afraid to try new things and throw yourself out of your comfort zone. I really sucked as a hostess on the first day, but I did get the hang of it slowly. Do not be afraid to make mistakes. It is okay to not be perfect at everything right away. Also, surround yourself as much as you can with people who align with you in mind, energy, and values.

You are so worthy, never settle.

A Letter of Self-Love

Can we stop lying to ourselves about being able to do everything at the same time? And lying to ourselves that we must "save" all our friends and everyone we know. When I say "save" I mean:

- Never saying no

- Always trying to fix everyone else

- Trying to convince others to believe what you believe

- Taking on extra work you know you can't handle

- Trying to accomplish everything at the same time

STOP!

This is permission to take a breath and re-evaluate every part of your life. You don't need to run on autopilot. You don't need to try to solve every problem for your friend or always play therapist.

You need to start taking care of yourself.

You need to start loving you.

You don't need to take on everyone's problems as your own.

You do need to take things one step at a time and try not to rush things.

Stop running. Start breathing. Start living. Stop sleeping. Wake up.

You can totally turn your life around.

One day at a time.

You are capable of anything.

Stop trying to be the hero and just focus on thriving. This will help others around you.

This will inspire others to turn their lives around.

I love you and you are loved. You are worthy.

My challenge is for you to write yourself a self-love letter! Post it on IG and tag me @danifeltinspires #selfloveletter. We all could use a little more self-love, am I right?

The Power of Being You

Never underestimate the power your music has on others' lives. Music heals. Music empowers. Music is everything. Music is your gift. Use your gift to spread love, joy, healing, empowerment, etc. You never know the difference your music will make in someone's life. The world needs your voice.

The Power of Saying No

Ugh! Saying no can suck sometimes. I get it! I hear you! But being able to tell people no is such a vital part to being a successful business person! We do not want to hurt our friend's feelings, we do not want to turn down an opportunity, but if something barely pays, is it really worth it? If someone crosses a boundary, and it makes you deeply uncomfortable that your body becomes full of resentment for that person, is it really worth not saying anything? When it comes to being an entrepreneur, saying no builds our power! It helps us level up.

I had people submit songs to me for a film opportunity. Some of the people did not meet the deadlines I had given them. I understand things happen, but when it comes to deadlines for getting music into TV and film, it is imperative to follow the deadline to a "T." Sometimes with pitches, I am only limited to a few songs and with this opportunity, it was three songs max. Since some people submitted past the deadline, I had to prioritize people who respected the deadline. If I tried submitting music to a sync agent past a deadline, it would be disrespecting the sync agent's time. It is so important to listen to the boundaries set by the people you are working for. My goal is to build great relationships with everyone I work with. The better relationships I build and the more respectful I am to people, the more it will also benefit my clients.

Now, I found three great songs and went with what I felt would make sense. At that point, it didn't make sense to spend more time or energy finding other songs. I need mutual respect from everyone. If I tell you something is closed, please do not email me asking me to still send it or to send your song anyway. This is my boundary. No means no.

I also noticed some of the artists text me about it. Unless we are good friends and hang out outside of work, it is important for me to have strong boundaries with this and communicate with people about business only via email. My exception is if someone's a paying client or a great friend of mine that I talk to on a weekly basis. If I do not know someone super well, I much rather they email me about business inquiries. The more boundaries I can implement, the more it will protect my mental energy. Hopefully, this inspires you to create more boundaries in your own life.

This Chapter Is Sponsored By

Upstream Artists
www.upstreamartists.com

Chapter 6

Lead Yourself Before You Lead Anyone Else

I would like to make an obvious statement. Being a leader is not about being a follower. This means, if you want to lead, you need to lead yourself first and make moves you believe are right for you. When we only listen to other people, we get unclear about what we actually want. It is easy to let people tell us what to do or make decisions for us. But at the end of the day, if we do not at least try to go for our dreams, we will have regret and resentment. Listening to our intuition, quieting our mind, creating space for things to come to us, working with people in alignment, investing into something when it feels right, these are all leadership for ourselves.

How can we lead others if we cannot lead ourselves, right? Leadership takes courage, strength, heart, wisdom—a bit like in the Wizard of Oz adventures. Sometimes, coaches can help guide us or share ideas with us, but it is important to get really clear on what we want and follow that. It is about what makes your heart sing, what inspires you, what motivates or drives you, what your core values are, what feels good in your body, versus what stresses you out to the point that you cannot even focus. Some level of stress is okay but if someone is constantly stressing you out, that's not good for you. Walk away from things or people that are not serving you.

Learn to lead yourself, one step at a time. Being a leader, you cannot expect everyone to believe you, or follow you, or listen to you, or agree with you. Do not pattern the way you live your life on others wanting you to go the safe route in your career, love life, etc. Do what feels right for you because the only person that can really guide you is yourself, and the universe, or your guides, etc.

People guide you based on their own biases, experiences, stories, emotions, and what works for them. Remember that we all have our own journey, and what works great for one person might not work great for another. So start quieting your mind a bit more and leave space to really get clear on what you want. Start leading yourself and the right people will follow your tribe. Do not worry about the rest. Remember, leadership starts with you leading yourself, not following.

Hero Versus Co-creator

I had a powerful realization as I was speaking with a friend. I find myself in a constant role of playing the hero. That means wanting to save people. A calling to feel that I have to save the world. However, I realized this frame of mind stems from fear not empowerment.

I think, as humans, we have a tendency to want to control the people in our lives. We sometimes use guilt, force, pushing, convincing, etc. However, what I came to realize was that everything is about co-creating. In other words, the energy of creation has to be one or more parties coming together to create a result or fulfill a goal. For example, if you are a songwriter, you are co-writing with someone else or co-creating with the universe, guides, God, higher self, your inspiration, your heart, your soul, or whatever you want to believe. To create, there always has to be more than one party, more than one energy at play, merging their energy to your energy.

If you have one person who does not want to do something and another person who really does, you create resistance. This is why the energy of convincing, forcing, pushing, manipulating, or trying to use fear creates blocks towards what that person is going for. In order for something to line up, it has to be in alignment. You need two people or two energies to create everything. For example, if you are a producer, you are co-creating the relationship and music with the artist. If the artist is not on the same page, resistance will occur. If you are coaching a client for business and the client does not want to do that thing, you are creating resistance and it will never work.

If you want to have a relationship with someone and you are always making an effort but the other person does not want that friendship, then there are going to be blocks towards building that friendship. If you have very strong beliefs and try to force them on someone else and they do not resonate with those beliefs, you are going to create resistance and they will be pushed away, not intrigued. In order for something to work, it has to be two energies on the same page. That is why it is important for you to get clear about whatever you want in your life and then align with the people who match those desires.

If you want to be a pop artist and only know hip hop producers and those hip hop producers do not want to learn pop music, then you need to find a pop producer. If you have a client who you have to beg to pay you or does not seem to want to work with you, I encourage you to drop them. Give them the option. Do not force things on people because you are setting yourself up for failure. Stay focused on what you want and find people who want that too.

This goes into the hero versus co-creator. So I think my entire life, I grew up learning to be the hero and saving everyone. Every time someone says negative things, I explain to them they need to change or else their life will suck. It was as if I could not just sit and watch someone be in pain or unhappy. I always felt I had to fix it. But the thing is, people will usually ask for help if they really want it. And when we force people to change or fix them, it will backfire because they do not want the help. So I have decided to create the intention to shift from being a hero to being a co-creator, aligning with the right people who want to accomplish a certain goal such as sync, services, etc.

I am here for you to empower you, inspire you, and hold space for you to co-create and amplify magic in your life. I encourage you to look at your life and see where you are playing the hero versus the co-creator and the shifts you might want to make in the roles you play in people's lives.

Listen to Your Heart

I truly enjoy inspiring and empowering you as a creative person. I believe in divine timing and I believe things happen for a reason. I believe there is a time for everything to transform. Like when I felt a very strong message to take a back seat to sync. Sync is something I have put so much energy and time into, but it has also caused me the most stress. It has triggered me to act a bit of a maniac at times when that is not my true nature.

As someone with ADHD, Facebook can also quite easily distract me when I see every post about a different sync, or a songwriting or singing opportunity which causes a lot of FOMO (fear of missing out) in me. So I think to myself, I must also post something! Nevertheless, I believe if something is meant for us, it will work out.

I also believe in this thing called balance and making sure our mental health is on point. Sometimes, we take on way more than we can handle because we think we are supposed to play the hero. False. This is a myth. Let me tell you, we are not meant to do everything and save the world. We are all here for a purpose, on this planet for a reason, but it is not to be everything to everyone. Trust me, trust me, trust me.

We have to learn to set boundaries. Sometimes, we have to say no. It is safe to turn down projects. If someone gets upset with us, that is on them, not us. We have the right to say no, to do what works best for us, and to have strong boundaries. All that being said, I realized I am doing way too much and part of that has been the amount of energy I am spending on looking for opportunities, songwriting, session singing, jobs, internships, and sync.

Transformation is inevitable. I want to focus my time and energy where it can be of the most value for both my clients and myself. The more successful I am, the more I will be able to help everyone in the long term. And be in an even more powerful position to impact the world with positivity, love, and inspiration. For those who want to continue to be along for the ride, look forward to creating some serious powerful transformation in your lives.

Step Into Your Power

Power. Sometimes, we don't feel we have any or we feel we lost it. We feel we don't have control. I'm here to tell you, we have more power than we think. Our power lies in the everyday choices we make. Who we let into our world. Who we confide things to. Who we bring on to our team. Who we collaborate creatively with. Who we choose as our friends. Who we choose as our coaches. What amount to pay them. What standards we hold for them. Who we take on as clients. How much we go out of our way for our clients. Who we introduce our clients to. What people we recommend to others. What our boundaries are. How we want people to treat us. How we react when people cross our boundaries or trigger us. It all lies in the everyday choices, so if you aren't happy with something, you have the power to shift it by deciding on a new choice.

Our power also lies in the stories we tell ourselves every day. Stories about our worth, that we only deserve to get paid X amount because we only have X experience. That we are only worthy of clients that need us on a certain level. Scarcity mindset: That we need X person to do Y task versus abundance mindset: There are plenty of people to complete a task and if X can't do it, another person can! We set the standards of how people treat us.

What choices can you start to make to create shifts in your life?

Affirmations

- Success is my story.

- I am worthy of getting paid.

- I'm worthy for just being born.

- I work and call in the best in all aspects of my life.

- I attract soulmate clients.

Top Tips

1. If you want to become a good leader, start with leading yourself.

2. Understand that people are telling you their opinions based on their own perspectives and experiences. At the end of the day, you have to do what works best for you.

3. When you recognize you are being the hero not the co-creator, pause and reflect. Is this the role you want to continue playing in this person's life?

4. Figure out what you want to do and do not want to do. Learn how to say no, so you do not take on more than you feel comfortable. "No" is a complete sentence.

5. When you feel out of alignment, step back into your power. Know that you have the ability to transform your life. It all starts with your beliefs.

6. If you want to practice exercising your power, practice making decisions.

7. Choose the story you want to tell yourself.

Lessons Learned

1. Just because someone is leading you does not make them a good leader.

2. People will not always agree with what we feel is best for us and that is okay.

3. Great coaches guide people and help people step into their own leadership and power.

4. If you want to become more powerful, learn how to step out of co-dependency and let people live their own lives.

5. The more we let go of control of others, the happier we will be.

6. Things will be in alignment when two people are co-creating with intention on a project.

7. Setting boundaries helps us step into our power and self-love.

8. Take back your power. It all starts with one action step and mindset shift at a time.

This Chapter Is Sponsored By

Brownie Marie
Founder of Life Entertainment News
www.lifeentertainmentnews.com

Chapter 7

Money Isn't the Problem, Your Story About It Is

Tapping Into Your Magic

How do you tap into your magic? If you want more money, start talking to money. Simple. Why? Because money is a form of energy, not just a physical material. Everything has energy and money is no different. Trust me, I learned this from millionaire coaches. When you understand the laws of energetics, you are able to become magic. As an experiment just for fun, I invite you to say the words, "Money, I am ready to have fun with you. Let's do this." When I said those words that day, one of my clients purchased my course and I saw one of my fans purchase my single "Unapologetic" on Bandcamp for $15. About ten other wins happened the same day. I was like, okay, this is the key!

Connecting to Abundance

As one of my coaches told me, you are the wealth of the universe individualized. Really think about that. How will you get there?

1. Visualize it.

2. Take actions steps towards it.

3. Feel into it.

4. Connect your emotions of joy and gratitude to whatever it is you desire.

5. Meditate on it.

6. Surround yourself with people who are doing what you want to do or going where you want to go.

Abundance Affirmations

- I am worthy of receiving abundance.

- I am looking forward to receiving money every day in many ways.

- Every day more and more abundance comes my way!

- There are unlimited opportunities for me and I get to choose which ones I want to take!

Speaking to Money Affirmations

- Money loves me and I love money.

- Money, I can't wait to have fun together!

- Money, let's make magic!

- Money, you are my best friend!

- Money, I know you are everywhere and will always be there for me!

- Money has my back!

- I am receiving so much money I need to open up a second account!

- I am receiving so much money I have to hire an assistant.

5 Tips for Receiving More Money

1. Know your worth. You see, if you undervalue yourself and settle, you will receive just that. Average in different parts of your life. Knowing your worth means having major self-respect. Turning down opportunities or invites when they don't feel good to you and having prices that make you feel good. After all, if you do not feel confident, safe, or good telling people your prices, why would others feel good about paying you? It all starts with your mindset.

2. Understand the law of what you give, you will receive. What you put out, you will get back. How you treat others will reflect how people will treat you. Say, you are holding on to money fiercely as if you would never receive money again. Holding on in fear and in a lack mindset thinking, "OMG, what if I don't get anymore? I can't spend more money! I must hold onto this!" When you think like this, you attract clients, fans, people, or friends, etc. who will also reflect this onto you.

   For example, if you feel anxiety when you spend money or pay for something and almost want to take it back right away, you will attract people who will feel the same when paying you. Start paying attention to what people do in your life when it comes to paying you, etc. as that will be a clear indicator of your own relationship with money. Look at everyone in your life like a complete mirror.

3. Start doing whatever you can possibly do at this time to feel good. Why? Because when you feel good, you are able to attract things at a higher vibration. Meaning, better opportunities, people, jobs, careers, relationships, and so on. You want money so bad and you are feeling really stressed? That is going to keep you stuck in a cycle of lack and will not help you bring more money into your life. Trust me, that will only keep you in a vicious cycle of lack of money. The better you feel, the more money you will naturally attract into your life. Try it and watch what happens! Get out of the victim mentality and play games. When was the last time you did something that made you feel good? Get on it!

4. Get clear on what amount of money you would like to receive. Do you want $5 every day? Do you want to bring in an extra $5,000 weekly? Do you want to become a multimillionaire? What do you want? It seems like a simple question but many of you have been trained or programmed to only think you know what you want, but that is actually what others want for you, not what you truly desire. Some of us have a lot of shame and guilt around wanting more money, because others might not have it. So we feel this, poor everyone else. How can I get this if others don't?

   If you think you want something, but deep down in your subconscious, you actually do not, there is going to be a mismatch of your energy. Therefore, you will not be able to call it into your life. Common reasons are subconscious fear, indecisiveness, or confusion. Sometimes, people are actually not sure what they want versus what society wants for them. So really sit down with your inner thoughts and feel into it. Place your hand on your heart and say to yourself, "Self, what do I actually want? Do I want to be super rich or am I actually terrified that if I am super rich, all my friends will take advantage of me or I will somehow lose that money, etc." The deeper you know yourself, the clearer you become on what you want. Thus, the stronger the energy you will hold to bring it to you.

5. Gratitude is a huge key for receiving more! When you are grateful, you step into the energy of gratitude and then you will receive so much more. If you are over here having a pity party and wondering where is the money and why isn't it more a part of your life, ask yourself these: When was the last time you gave thanks to money? When was the last time you wrote down a list of things you are grateful for? When was the last time you showed appreciation to the people in your life that go out of their way to help you in any and all capacities?

When you really sit back and think about it, you will realize how much you do have. So if you want more money, start being grateful and write out a small list of five to ten things that you are grateful for. It could be as simple as the sun, or that new job promotion, or for your amazing friends, and even for having the chance to record and write your last single.

Whether you are an artist, producer, or any creative professional, at the end of the day, you are running your own business. Now, the energetics of money is one small part but so is aligned pricing, sales skills, ability to monetize everything you are doing, having a strong social media presence that makes it super clear who you are, who you serve and what you do, having strong call to actions, having great giveaways to attract new clients, and of course, the whole mindset and getting out of your own way, identifying and letting go of fears, having the right products and services, and more are all important aspects of running a business.

10 Ways to Bring More Abundance Into Your Life

1. Make a list of what you want to bring into your life and write it down saying, I am or I have, etc. Make sure to write it in the present. For example, instead of "I want a client," write "I am receiving clients." Whatever amount of money you want to bring into your life, make a spreadsheet list of what amount you will spend on what.

2. Get a blank check and write the amount you want to bring into your life and where you want the money to come from. For example, if you are a producer, write the amount on the check or a piece of paper and write from production services. My client did this and received even more than he wrote out.

3. Make a vision board and post on it what you want to bring into your life. Use photos, words, or stickers. You can even make one on Pinterest.

4. Write out a list of the things you're grateful for that you want to happen; such as, I am so happy and grateful for getting new production clients, etc. :)

5. Visualize what you want to bring into your life. If you can visualize it, you can bring it into existence.

6. Have more fun. The more fun you have, the more money you will receive!

7. Listen to meditations or things that help you stay in a balanced state of mind. When you feel good, you will bring more opportunities into your life. Focus on your mental health.

8. Drop anyone who does not support your dreams. You will make the amount of money of the average income of the five people you hang out with the most.

9. Write down daily wins and celebrate them! The more wins you celebrate, the more of it you will bring into your life.

10. Lastly, play with what is possible versus what is logical. Dream big and play the "what if" game.

Fun and Playfulness

Sometimes, you just gotta embrace having more fun in your life and be more playful, in general, because we can get so caught up in the mundane, or the to-do lists. etc. I encourage you to just start asking yourself, how can I bring more joy into my life? You see, joy is one of the keys to happiness. It can be so easy to go down a rabbit hole of social media posts filled with dark, dark energy and intensity that can fill our hearts and minds with depression and doomsday mentality.

Remember that what we focus on, we are also attracted to. So the more we focus on the "reality" of every situation in the darkest way, the more we are attracted to it. TV is "programming." Whatever you watch, you focus on. So really start to think, how can I bring more joy into my life? What am I focusing my time on and what are my thoughts focused on? What stories am I telling myself today? Am I telling myself the world is doomed? Or am I telling myself, I am doing the best I can do every day and that is the only control I have?

If each of us can just focus on doing what we can to protect our mental health and start embedding small things into our lives that bring us joy, think about how big the impact it could make to society. Plus, our life is a total mirror. If you are focused on what is going wrong, you will find yourself attracting more and more people who also focus on this. But if you focus on the joy, you can see even the smallest things that can bring happiness—a funny laugh, a beautiful flower outside, delicious cookies or desserts, the smell of the rain or shower, a beautiful song that makes you cry, and more. Focus on the joy!

Lessons Learned

- Money is a form of energy and it's important to build a relationship with it.

- The more fun you have, the more money will come into your life. Money loves to be around fun!

- The more grateful you are, the more you will receive!

- When you get more specific on what you want to receive and the amount, you will have an easier time attracting it.

- When you get clear on what you want to spend your money on, your subconscious mind will have an easier time getting behind it.

- Fear is one of the biggest reasons we do not receive as much as we want. We must work with our subconscious mind to get behind what we want.

- The better you feel, the higher vibration you will be in, and the more money you will attract.

- What you give, you will also receive. So give graciously.

Make It Easy to Get Paid

Make it easy for your clients to pay you. Ask them to do the following:

- Engage with my social media content! Like, love, comment, save, and share.

- Share on your stories about my brand and tag me.

- Invite your friends to follow me on my socials.

- Join my mailing list.

- Subscribe to my YouTube channel.

- Purchase my merch.

- Attend events I host, live or virtual.

- Watch and/or share any interviews I do.

- Venmo, cash app, or PayPal me for any amount.

- If I ever launch a Patreon, become a Patron.

- If I ever launch a Kickstarter or Indiegogo campaign, support me.

- Share my content with your mailing list.

- Invite me to do an interview or an IG Live.

This Chapter Is Sponsored By

**Jourdan Rystrom
Singer/Songwriter, Hypnotherapist,
Empowerment Coach,
and Founder of Awaken the Glow
www.linktr.ee/jourdanrystrom**

Chapter 8

Relationships: Where Your Patterns Get Loud

Power of Proximity

Remember that who you surround yourself with is key to your greatest success. Your relationships are gold. Don't be fooled and think that the people in your life are separate from you. At the end of the day, everything is connected and you never know why someone comes into your life at that moment. You never know who that person in your life is going to connect you with to help you go on that next step to embrace your new journey, so be open-minded.

We may not see the reason right away but I believe everything happens for a reason. Sometimes, the reason is to bring to the forefront things that people don't really want to talk about. Sometimes, things happen to teach us lessons. Sometimes, it's karmic. It all depends. But I guarantee you, when you look at your life, everything is interconnected. It is one giant puzzle. So embrace the unknown and dive deep into the adventure.

Secrets to Success

1. Surround yourself with the right people. Make sure you are around people who are supportive of your dreams. This is a huge key. Anyone who doubts your dreams or reflects any negativity through their own insecurities and fears, let them go.

2. Take the right action steps. You can't just close your eyes and hope your dreams come true. You need to take action, the right power moves. Figure out where you want to go then take one step at a time to get there. Micro steps, if you will. For example, with my TV show: First, we wrote out ideas. Then, we wrote out a pitch deck and one sheet. Then, we found a team to film the trailer, etc. Take it one step at a time. Rome was not built in a day and neither will your dreams.

3. Learn to lead yourself. By leading yourself, you will in fact empower others to lead themselves. Ask yourself, what do I truly want, deep down? Then go for it!

4. Take risks. Don't be afraid to make mistakes, to fall down and try again. Don't be afraid to fail. You will never know unless you try. Put yourself out there. Don't be afraid to be vulnerable. On the other side of fear are all our dreams.

5. Create the right strategic partnerships. Team up with others, find people who will refer you. Find people who will barter with you, create win-wins so everyone is happy. None of us are meant to accomplish our dreams alone.

6. Visualize your dreams in your mind. Over and over again, play out what you want to see happen. If you can see it, you can create it.

7. Lastly, be aware of what you feed your mind with. It is in your control what you choose to focus on, the messages in the music you tune into, the friends you choose to hang out with, the TV shows you choose to watch, the places you choose to go to eat and drink, etc. All these tiny daily decisions create a huge effect and impact on where you are headed. Every choice creates a new path. Are you choosing to listen to positive and inspirational podcasts and people and what's possible, or tuning into the "logical" world and forgetting the world of possibility? No one successful was a realist. They all challenged the impossible. Just saying.

Do not try to force anything. The more you push, the more resistance you will create. Flow, go with it. When something does not work out, let it be. Whatever is meant for you will work out, trust me. Stop doubting your own abilities and start living up to your potential. Now is the time to try. Now is the time to take action. Now is the time to build your team. Who is on your team? These people are key. Building the right team is key. Knowing the people, who know the right people to help support your dreams, and have aligned vision and goals with you are key to your own success and happiness.

Not that happiness is driven by success but being around the right people will make all the difference. Start building your team. Let go of people who are not for your dreams. Let go of people who hold you back, who create doubt in your mind, who tell you to be realistic. When we let go of things, we create space for new things. Trust me.

Back in 2024, I met up with this guy named Evan Stein. I met Evan through a friend who introduced us because he was looking for a lyric video for one of his clients. I started slowly having him do consulting sessions related to branding with my clients. A few months later, I flew to LA for my birthday week to see if I truly wanted to move there. That was one of the best birthday weeks ever, so many things fell in line. Evan Stein was one of the people I decided to meet in person. He has had hundreds of placements getting music into huge films and shows. I felt it would be a smart move to meet with him. Never underestimate the power of meeting someone in person, even for coffee.

Evan explained that he wanted me to get more involved with his company and what he is doing for artists. He also introduced me to a music supervisor, an artist who does showcases in Nashville, and more. The fact that Evan went out of his way to introduce me to other people to help me, said a lot. Therefore, I decided to bring him on board to help my clients with branding. It is so important to team up with the right people and bring people on your team who complement you. Months later, I ended up moving to LA, and before you knew it, Evan and I were speaking on stage together at music colleges. Like I said, never underestimate the power of one meeting. Evan and I continue to work together helping artists build their brand and share their story in a powerful way.

What has building relationships for years helped me achieve thus far?

- One of my sync agency contacts got a client's song I submitted placed for a client in the Nancy Drew show on CW.

- I have been featured on many podcasts to share my message due to my constant hustle of reaching out.

- I got one of my clients an opportunity to compose for an online TV show.

- A music supervisor reached out to me for music and placed two of my clients' music in a movie.

- I hosted a music blog which featured over three hundred people and turned it into a book. In that book, we got to interview people like Lou, founder of ReverbNation; Benji Rogers, ex-CEO of Pledgemusic; Poo Bear, a producer that works with Justin Bieber often; Trevor Gale, ex-VP of SESAC, and more.

- I went to NAMM (National Association of Music Merchants) and met the right manager for one of my clients who submitted his music to a label in seconds.

- I submitted another client to a manager and he picked her up.

- I got the opportunity to co-write an artist's song due to my relationship with the producer.

Do you want to know one of my biggest secrets to success? The ability to be clear on my vision, believe in myself, build relationships, and take action steps towards my dreams. You can do anything; it just takes one step at a time.

The Friendship Guide

If you want to be my friend, this is a good guide! Honestly, I encourage you to do this with people in your life so they understand you better. Communication is everything.

Biggest ways to show you care about people:

1. Say thank you; appreciation goes a long way!

2. Reach out to someone. Just to say "hi" without asking for anything.

3. Compliment people! People love compliments!

4. Tell them they are doing a great job with whatever you hired them for.

5. Like or engage with their social media posts, stories, reels, etc.

6. Invite them to hang out to see a show, attend an event, etc.

7. Listen when they are speaking to you and ask questions if you do not understand something.

This can be people's biggest triggers:

1. When someone ignores a question or message.

2. When someone is super negative.

3. When someone starts complaining.

4. When someone tells their friend they will do something, then does not, or any broken promises.

5. When someone says one thing then changes their mind.

6. When someone asks your friend who they know and to introduce everyone they know to them.

If you want to communicate with friends about something:

1. Tell them when something is bothering you or if you feel they crossed a boundary because otherwise they will not always know.

2. Be very specific when you want them to do something, like meetings, tasks, etc., otherwise, they will have a million questions in their head.

3. It is possible your friends could act a lot quieter around groups than when one-on-one so if you want to hear them speak a lot, meet with them on Zoom or alone in person.

Communication method preferences:

1. Text! But do not text them 24/7! They could get annoyed if they feel someone is wasting their time just because you are bored.

2. You can also call them but I advise not calling them super early because they will most likely want that time to themselves.

3. Please do not call them directly if you are looking to be a potential client, just book a call with them for this.

Fastest ways to win points with people:

1. Be really talented at something.

2. Be really driven.

3. Be an optimistic person.

4. Send good vibes to others.

5. Be kind.

6. Introduce them to other people!

Fastest ways to be blocked:

1. Make inappropriate comments.

2. Ask them about sending you money.

3. Ask them about buying promotional services.

4. Leave multiple comments on one post.

5. Message them multiple messages, multiple times a day that have no point, such as sending them weird GIFs.

Customer Service Needs Empathy

A specific situation I have gone through bothered me so much subconsciously. So much so, that I started writing a draft text to the assistant of this business owner to speak my mind. I was at a business and had the most jarring experience with a business owner. I experienced what it is like to be a client for a non-empathetic business owner and it freaking hurts emotionally, spiritually, mentally, etc.

When you are a business owner, pretty much anyone that does anything related to making money, there is a certain skill that is required in order to make you a better business owner, and that is empathy and caring about your clients. Now, I understand that not everyone is the most sensitive or shows emotions but there has to be a balance. If you come off as cold, harsh, insensitive, or like you do not care whatsoever, you are going to turn clients off and they are never going to want to work with you again. Be kind to humans. Treat them like gold. These humans are your fans and clients and they do not want to be treated like just a number.

At the end of the day, we all need to eat but we can still do that with mutual respect for the people that are hiring us for any and all services, including fans who buy your merchandise or stream your music. Also, pretend that every human you know, that you interact with, especially your clients, knows at least a thousand people so they can make or break your business. Make sure to treat them all like VIPs in your book!

So in life, when we are triggered by something, it is usually a mirror. That is why it bothers us so much, because it reminds us of something we do not want to face about ourselves. So I asked myself, have I ever treated someone like they are just a number? Have I ever lacked empathy when dealing with clients? Where in my life can I show more empathy or sensitivity to others? Maybe I come off like I do not care and only care about making money, and if that is the case, I sincerely apologize. Because I truly do care and would never want anyone to feel like how I felt working with this specific business, basically on the verge of tears!

We all deserve to be treated like gold. So, next time you work with clients, please remember to be sensitive to them, be kind, and practice empathy. Really try to view everyone with respect and love. This is so important and you never know how one person, like a super fan, can help elevate your business to the next level. It can be easy to take people for granted unintentionally.

So what did I do? I decided to first, send them a text message explaining to the assistant how I felt and why I felt the way I did. Second, I decided to never go back there. So I told the assistant I will be looking for other people who can help me and that it just was not a match. After I did this, I totally cried and felt relief, my soul was cheering. It is amazing how, when you release certain people in your life, how much better you feel! Please just keep my story in mind when you are selecting who you want to hire for everything, from hair salons, medical, business, marketing, to managers. Make sure whoever you choose makes you feel good, understands you, and has the best intentions for you.

And remember if you ever feel negativity, or a weird vibe, or not good around someone, you have the freedom to walk away! I believe everyone should spend as much time as possible with those who make them feel good, raise them up, and are supportive. We all have a choice on who we choose to hire and make sure it lines up with our values. And always practice empathy for your clients and to try to walk in their shoes. Just be kind, it's really not that hard. :D

Here's another story that happened to me that I feel could be a learning lesson to you as an artist, entrepreneur, producer, CEO of a company, or something else, when it comes to treating your clients or customers right. It was an ordinary day in the City of Nashville when I decided it would be a good idea to go get an eye exam so I could get my glasses that I scratched replaced with new lenses. I walked in the store and met the customer service reps then I did the eye exam. The doctor, a very older man, got extremely close to my face as I was being examined. I felt like my space was invaded but did not know how to say something without offending him.

Eventually, I walked out of the exam room and went to talk to the customer service reps again to check out for my eye exam. As I sat down, they mentioned to me that my glasses are impossible to fix because they are old; the frame needs to be replaced. I thought about it and was excited to see the new glasses options. So I asked the customer service rep, "What are your nicest glasses?" The customer service rep pointed to a corner and replied, "Well, the cheapest ones are over in that corner." I repeated, I do not care about cheap, I want nice. I work in music and I need to look good for my brand. Another customer rep spoke up this time and mentioned several other possible areas that I could look across the room but then again mentioned the cheaper options.

Now granted, I never mentioned I wanted cheap, and even hinted I wanted nice over cheap. Normally, I love to shop and invest in stores. I love to give people my money and buy things that make me happy. But these customer service reps did not seem to care about me or the money I was willing to spend to get a product I was happy with. I hinted that I wanted help to find the perfect glasses to match my brand, but the customer service reps seemed to not really care and just lazily pointed around the store saying to feel free to look around and just try things out.

This was not the customer service experience I had dreamed of. So I decided, instead of investing into this store which seemed to care less about taking my money, I got my new prescription from the eye exam I had just taken and only paid for that. I thought to myself, I am sure there are other stores that will happily help me and gladly want me to spend money on their products.

Lessons Learned

1. Your customers, fans, or clients are everything. Without them, you have no business. Make sure to show them you appreciate and care about them. Sometimes, it is even good to go out of your way to make your business stand out. You can do this by sending them cards, gifts, or thank you emails. You can also throw in something extra for them in your services, give them a shout out on social media, showcase them on your website, etc.

2. If you want to attract more clients and fans, make a list of what their personality is like and what they are into.

3. There is so much competition out there, make sure to be kind to your clients. Show them you actually care about them and that you like working together. If you are not nice to your clients, they can leave you and work with other people that offer the same services as you.

4. Make sure to go out of your way to help your clients. Do not assume they just know what they're doing. Especially if this is about purchasing from you, make it easy for them to buy from you.

5. Be an active listener. Make sure to listen to your clients

carefully and read between the lines about what they want. You could even go further by researching them on social media to learn more about them. Think of this like searching for music supervisors—looking up their social media to see the way they speak, what they care about, what projects they are working on, etc.

6. Be friendly! Being friendly goes a long way. People can feel the vibration, good energy, and good attitudes. Bringing in a friendly attitude to every potential customer will help increase your chances of sales. It is very simple, just be positive.

7. If you, for some reason, are in a bad mood that day, at least pretend you still care. It will make or break your sales and make a difference to get repeat customers.

8. Show your clients, customers, or fans respect and that you value them as people.

Affirmations

- The kindness I show others will return to me tenfold.

- The right people always show up in the perfect divine timing.

- Only people in alignment with me will show up.

- I release anyone who does not have my greatest intention and I create new space for people who are in alignment with me.

- I attract people who respect me, appreciate me, and love me.

- I work with the best people.

- I attract my soulmate clients.

This Chapter Is Sponsored By

Calvin Lawrence Speaks
www.calvinlawrencespeaks.net

Chapter 9

Rewrite the Story.
You're the Author Now

Changing Your Story

I think I cracked the code. It all starts with how you view yourself, your offers, your time, and your value. Once you see the value you offer, something starts to shift big time. All of a sudden, the world starts reflecting back at you what you believe in yourself. How are you seeing yourself every day? Are you visualizing the person you truly want to become or are you seeing yourself as struggling, frustrated, etc.?

The best news is that you can start making changes in your life today. You can start waking up with a more positive attitude. You can choose how you react to and view a situation. If that client did not sign with you, maybe they were not the right fit for you, and that is okay. There are more than enough people out there that would love to work with you for being you. So, the next time you have doubts about your own abilities, ask yourself what story you are telling yourself about you every day. Can you shift that by telling yourself a more positive story?

Can you be a little kinder to yourself and appreciate how far you have come?

Small Changes Equal Big Results

Do you want to make changes in your life? Let me tell you a secret.

Are you ready?

The secret to making changes in your life is… making changes in your life! I know it's crazy, right?!

What does this mean exactly? It means you cannot make changes in your future by focusing on the current version of yourself right now. The way to bring changes in your life is to start making decisions based on the future version of yourself, the best version of yourself you could possibly imagine.

What would you do and say, and how would you act, think, hang around, charge pricing, or sell, as the future version of yourself that you desire to become? Would that Grammy-winning version of you really focus so much on the petty drama? Would that version focus on worrying about money or opportunities? Would that person constantly create drama for attention, or to self-sabotage, or because they're scared of actually failing? Or would that version be focusing on how incredible their life is, how happy they are? Would they surround themselves with people who tell them life sucks and is hard and it's impossible to accomplish your dreams? Or would that version of yourself surround themselves with people who are happy, supportive, inspiring, empowering, driven?

The secret to making a change in your life is to start taking action from that place. Wake up every day with the perspective that you already are that person you want to become. You have already won Grammys. You already are working with top producers. You already have that amazing manager or dream client. When you speak from that place and live your life from that place, that is when your life will start to transform.

Limiting Beliefs

I know you have big dreams and big visions for yourself and I totally believe you can do anything. However, sometimes it just takes some adjustments and tweaks to get where we want to go. Here is a list of the top ten things that can stop you from achieving your dreams. I also added the last one as a bonus:

1. Self-doubt

2. Lack of self-worth

3. Perfectionism

4. Information overload

5. Competition over collaboration

6. Lack of the right relationships

7. Ego

8. Indecisiveness

9. Fear

10. People-pleasing

11. Lack of direction

How to move past any or all of these blocks:

1. Read books on it.

2. Watch YouTube videos.

3. Google it.

4. Ask friends in Facebook groups.

5. Buy online courses.

6. Hire a coach.

What is the value of working with a coach to help you achieve your goals?

1. Keeps you accountable

2. Builds your confidence

3. Helps you get clear on your vision

4. Helps you develop strategies and a plan

5. Helps you create your brand

6. Helps you develop and price your offers

7. Helps you figure out your audience

8. Utilizes relationships to help you move further faster

9. Full support for you and your big dreams

Things to Journal On

- What would my future self look like?

- How would I speak?

- What words would I say?

- What actions would I take?

- Who would I spend time with?

- Where would I travel?

- What would my standards be for my life?

- What changes can I start implementing in my life to start seeing changes?

Career Affirmations

- I am living my dream life.

- I am doing my dream career.

- I love my life!

- I have so much joy doing what I do!

- I feel happy and satisfied with life!

- Life feels AMAZING!

- I am working for my dream people.

- I am working with my dream team!

- My team has my back!

- I am living my passion and purpose!

Affirmations to Attract Opportunities

- I am always attracting better and better opportunities in my life!

- My dream media outlet is featuring me!

- My dream client is hiring me!

- I am receiving my dream salary.

- I am receiving so many opportunities, I have to turn some down! I choose what I desire to do! I get to choose!

- I am booking my dream roles and gigs.

- I attract the right people to see my worth and give me aligned opportunities that feel good and are in my highest interest!

Taking Action

Write down the names of ten people you want to build stronger relationships with:

1.

2.

3

4.

5.

6.

7.

8.

9.

10.

Now select two of them and go contact them to schedule a plan to meet for coffee, a phone call, a Zoom call, etc.

This Chapter Is Sponsored By

Blayann Babes
www.blayannbabes.com

Jourdan Rystrom Music
www.linktr.ee/jourdanrystrom

Chapter 10

Your Gifts Aren't Random (They're Clues)

Understanding the reason for your why is everything. It can be the very essence of why you can feel motivated to jump out of bed. "Why do you get outta bed and why should anyone care?" This is a question a good colleague of mine, Evan Stein, had asked me to ponder one day. I had asked Evan to help me with building my brand for my own artistry. Dark pop, empowered, bold, courageous, and more. This was the first question he had me journal on. Hmmm, I had never thought of finding my why this way before. I realized at that moment how important this question is to reflect on when it comes to finding your why.

Sometimes, we think money is enough to motivate us. Sometimes, we get into business for this very reason, to bring in some side money to help us pay for whatever it is we want. However, when you are struggling and feel depressed, sometimes money is not enough. There have been many times when I felt super motivated to be a millionaire and was working hard to just hustle all the time. But I got so burnt out from this mentality; I could only keep the momentum for so long.

Then, I started falling into depression. I was watching myself scrolling on social media for hours. That's when I realized money was not enough of a reason to really motivate me to get out of bed and care.

Another week, a client told me how doing these branding sessions was like therapy and it has been transforming their life. Helping artists find their why and their purpose was life-changing for them. That same week, I had shown someone who was struggling, my podcast along with my manifesting course. I then decided to just gift her my course because I felt the call to help. Sometimes, it's not about money. Sometimes, it's about love, and kindness, and just helping people when we feel called to. I asked for a testimonial a few months later and she told me my course and podcast totally helped her so much.

A struggling actor who was trying to turn things around said my course and podcast helped her have a whole new perspective. I showed another girl my music and she said my music made her feel so empowered that she decided to hire me for a session. I asked myself, "Okay, what is the pattern between my podcast, courses, the branding I do with Evan, and my music?" It all came down to my why: Empowering other people. Being a force for good.

Money? Becoming a millionaire? Well, yes I still wanted that. But empowering others, being a resource for others, guiding others, connecting others to help them with their own path, this was my why. This became a light bulb moment in my life. I understood then why I have a podcast, have a company, do music, want to also build TV shows and films, it is all about empowering others.

Now, it is your turn to discover your why. Start with journaling the question, "Why do I get out of bed and why should anyone care?" Truly ask yourself, why do you do what you do? Why does it matter to you and why does it matter to others? Some examples could be empowering others, being a force to help those who need a hero, or be an advocate for mental health. Maybe it is just to keep achieving your dreams because no one ever believed in you as a child and you want to prove them wrong. It could be anything. There are no wrong or right answers.

I would love to share with you some of our clients' reasons why they do what they do to give you some examples to start thinking about.

Dani Felt's Mission Statement: To create emotionally raw, cinematic music that empowers people to embrace their authentic selves, heal through vulnerability, and break free from limiting beliefs.

Alina's Mission Statement: To create emotionally honest, empowering music that reflects vulnerability, self-worth, and healing; offering listeners a space to feel seen, inspired, and connected.

Piano Jordan's Mission Statement: To uplift, inspire, and bring people together through the power of music. With his soulful piano-driven melodies and heartfelt storytelling, he creates a space where joy, connection, and positivity thrive. Whether through original songs, collaborations, or interactive performances, Jordan's goal is to spread hope and unity through music.

Oda Rose's Mission Statement: To create authentic, uplifting music that celebrates love, personal growth, and the beauty in everyday moments, inspiring listeners to embrace their true selves and find joy in life's journey.

So start journaling on your why and see what unfolds!

Finding your why takes time. You have to dig deep. This is why Evan and I have an entire twelve-week branding program just to help artists and business owners understand their why, and build the entire foundation of their brand. From their brand archetype, colors, fonts, mission statement, vision statement, social media strategy, tone of voice and so much more.

Find Where You Fit

After I quit my first restaurant job as a hostess, I have decided that working in the restaurant industry is not my cup of tea or my strength. Turns out, I am not cut out to be either a hostess or a waitress. First of all, you have to be really physically strong! When I was training as a server, I almost dropped the second plate. I'm clearly not strong enough for this.

Second of all, you can fall really easily and I am a bit accident prone even with hopefully the right shoes. I even spilled water on a customer during training LOL. Know that you're never supposed to pour water over a customer! Third, everyone was like speed walking! And fourth of all, I felt like my set of skills was not very helpful there. Honestly, I went back and forth. Should I stay or should I go? Should I challenge myself or should I do something that comes easier to me?

At the end of the day, I decided I would rather do something that comes natural to me than push myself so physically hard just to prove to myself that I am capable. Managing my stress better and getting my health even stronger have been my goals. So I decided to go with the path of least resistance and asked my guides for a sign to show me the way. To show me if I am meant to do something part-time and who to work for. I then reached out to my latest contact and he agreed to let me try being his assistant. Scored a new opportunity!

My point is, we always have a choice to choose. Sometimes, we think we are stuck in a situation but there are unlimited opportunities when it comes to everything—job, relationship, career, clients, friendships. We do not have to feel stuck. There is always another option and that option could be even greater than you never imagined. And also you might not even have gotten to that option unless you took the chance of that other wrong option, so really it all leads you to somewhere. So my points are:

1. Do not be afraid to take chances.

2. Do not be afraid to make mistakes.

3. Do not be afraid to put yourself out there.

4. Do not be afraid to change your routine.

5. Do not be afraid to leave, quit, or walk away.

6. Do not be afraid to change your mind.

At the end of the day, you know what matters, so focus on what you want and not on what others tell you is right. They are only projecting their opinions on you. Even if you have to go for a walk, sit quietly, and meditate to get really clear on what you want. The more we try new things, the more it will help us get clear on what we do not want, which will in turn, lead us to know what we do want. When one door closes, it makes room for a new door to open. Do not be afraid to close a door and find a new door.

From this experience, I decided I love working from home. I love doing marketing, admin., etc. and do not like working in the restaurant world. There is always a lesson to be learned. I challenge you to go try something new! Learn more about what you like and do not like. Try new food, dance places, meet new people, go to an event, travel, etc. Put yourself out there and try switching some things up.

Taking Action

Write down ten things you want to try out:

1.

2.

3.

4.

5.

6.

7.

8.

9.

10.

Now select two of them and go try them!

-oOo-

Write down ten hobbies or activities that make you happy:

1.

2.

3.

4.

5.

6.

7.

8.

9.

10.

Now select two of them and schedule these weekly in your calendar!

-oOo-

Write down ten things you want to learn more about, or skills you want to improve:

1.

2.

3.

4.

5.

6.

7.

8.

9.

10.

Now select two of these and go find a class to learn them or ask your friends to teach you. It could be as small as learning a new recipe to as big as learning how to ride a mountain bike.

Write down ten of your best skills:

1.

2.

3.

4.

5.

6.

7.

8.

9.

10.

Now select the top three skills you enjoy the most and the three skills you are best at. Now start thinking about how you can use those skills to make money.

This Chapter Is Sponsored By

Steve Memel
Celebrity Voice and Performance Coach
www.stevenmemel.com

Chapter 11

Make the Plan. Then Actually Follow It

What is scary is that so many artists create music and spend hours recording and writing but then when it comes to marketing, they have no team, no plan, no strategy, and just expect their fans to magically show up! I am all about believing in miracles but let's be real, being an artist is a business. And many artists do not plan out their releases, they kinda just hope it will magically work!

The Power of Showing Up

I gotta say, even if someone is huge, do not be afraid to reach out! Seriously! Take all the chances! I received a letter from Selena Gomez's manager telling me she was not available for our show as a judge. I then realized it was because she was on "The Voice." I also received an email from two of the biggest supervisors in the music industry about my show; one said, "No, thank you," and one said, "Let's talk!" So never be afraid to go for the biggest people ever! You never know until you reach out!

Shifting Directions

When it comes to shifting directions, you have to ask yourself, "How am I feeling right now about the current situation I am in?" Ask yourself whether you are happy with where you work. Are you happy with the clients you work with? Are you happy with the amount of money you get paid? If not, ask yourself what you can do to start shifting that. Is it applying for new jobs? Is it raising your pricing? Is it becoming more scalable so that you don't have to work as much with people one-on-one? Is it building out a course so more people can access what you want to offer? Is it moving homes? Is it breaking up with that friend that is always speaking negatively about everything? What small shifts can you start to make to build a change in your path?

You know in life, I believe in my heart, we are guided and directed by the universe on our path. Things come into our life called blocks to show us new directions. Sometimes, the universe gives small whispers or hints and then it can become louder, and louder, and louder, and louder. Sometimes, the universe is literally screaming in our ears and we are so stubborn and refuse to listen. We refuse to look at truths, we refuse to acknowledge things.

I believe the universe has been giving me hints related to managing in sync. I believe things happen for a reason. I believe that when we are meant to do something, there will be clear signs in front of us. And you know, I was very stubborn about this. I told myself, "Dani, I know you just burned three bridges in one year with supervisors but you are learning so much. Keep going!" And do not get me wrong, I do love pitching songs for opportunities but I feel I did go a bit overboard. As a person with ADHD and born under the Pisces sign, I can get super passionate about something and then go full force.

My point is, when we feel called towards something, we go for it. I felt really called towards managing artists in sync for a while! And it has been an interesting adventure filled with many learning lessons. However, when I see the power in my coaching sessions with artists and the impact it makes in their lives, that is one of the most rewarding feelings ever. It just makes me feel a hundred times more fulfilled than just simply pitching music.

When people thank me for connecting them to my PR or video people, etc. and they thank me for the incredible results they got, that feels so good in my heart! When we feel good doing something, that is a clear sign that we are on the right path. Though, I do still find some fun opportunities and I will continue to pitch music when given a clear opportunity such as, "Hey, Dani, we need pop singers for X thing. Send me what you got." Sure, I have absolutely no problem doing that.

Why am I sharing this story with you? Well, I feel when I open up to people about my story, my perspective, what I am personally going through in my business, it also serves others and can give them a new perspective. So what is my point in this case? My point is, pay attention to signs and also what comes easily or naturally to you, in addition to what makes you happy.

What do you wake up excited to do? What do you spend hours, and hours, and hours, and hours doing that you could care less about the money? What would you continue to do anyway even if you are rich? And that answer for me is coaching, connecting artists to my team to help them professionally in all aspects of their career. This is what drove me to start my first blog over ten years ago, pursuing music as an artist.

When we are called towards something and we pursue that career, hobby, or passion, the universe will guide us and I am feeling very guided to somehow inspire you, to help you take action in your own life. You are amazing. You are powerful and you can do anything. Keep believing in your dreams and being a rockstar, badass, amazing human!

I love to work with people who are super passionate and are willing to take chances and invest in themselves. Because when you do, that is when things start to move, shift, transform, etc. When we stay in fear and stagnant energy, we stay in the lake and then things do not move or shift. So, if you are looking to take action in your career or are thinking about what steps you can take, look forward and see what makes sense for you.

I am not saying that hiring my team is the end all and be all. I am saying that investing in yourself as an artist is such a power move. It gives you more control in your path as an artist, especially when you do not have a label backing you. Now, if you are a producer, it could be more about willingness to invest in the right equipment for your clients, showing up, or creating content on social media. It is all an investment, whether it is time or money.

I would also encourage you to celebrate your wins and even better if you write them down. Because the act of celebration creates more, and more, and more of whatever it is that we received. So absolutely celebrate! It is so inspiring for me to see so much success within the music community!

Taking Action

Name ten things you want to change about yourself:

    1.

    2.

    3.

    4.

5.

6.

7.

8.

9.

10.

Now select two of those and create a call to action for that. If you want to become a more educated person, maybe the call to action is dedicating one day a week to listening to podcasts that inform you. If you want to get better with money, maybe it's hiring a coach to help you with finances, or maybe it's taking a course on finances, or maybe speaking to a friend who is really great with money and asking for some advice.

-oOo-

Write down 10 things you want to accomplish in the next twelve months:

1.

2.

3.

4.

5.

6.

7.

8.

9

10.

Now select two of them to hyper focus on. Then write down one step you are going to take towards that goal:

Goal 1

Microstep 1:

Goal 2

Microstep 1:

Now go do both! Keep repeating the next microstep after you do the first one!

For example:

Goal 1 Record an album

Microstep 1: Contact producer to setup a writing session with them.

In order to accomplish things, I believe it's important to focus on one small step at a time. As creatives and business owners, it can be easy to get lost in overwhelm when we have too many steps to do at once. Therefore, it is important to focus on one small step at a time for each goal. So start with 1 or 2 goals and focus on the first small step to take to reach them.

Alright now, it's time to look into things you want to improve. Write down ten habits or mindsets you want to shift or get rid of:

1.

2.

3.

4.

5.

6.

7.

8.

9.

10.

Now select your top two and write one microstep to accomplish it.

Habit 1

Microstep to get rid of habit 1:

Habit 2

Micro step to get rid of habit 2:

Example:

Habit 1 You want to decrease your time on social media.

Microstep example: Read one book a week.

Microstep example 2: Take a walk every day for ten minutes a day.

Microstep example 3: Dedicate one day a week to listen to a new podcast.

-oOo-

When it comes to making a plan, working with the right people is key. Write down ten people you want to connect with that will lead you closer to your goals:

1.

2.

3.

4.

5.

6.

7.

8.

9.

10.

Example 1: I want to produce a movie. I will connect with a director, a movie producer, a screenwriter, a fundraiser, a marketer, a casting director, etc.

Example 2: I want to produce an album. I will connect with someone who I can write with, a producer, a branding specialist, a social media manager, and more.

Example 3: I want to become a coach. I will connect with a coach to coach me, and reach out to nine potential clients.

Now select two of the people on your list and go reach out to them via email, call, or text to make a plan to meet with them either in person or virtually.

Branding

As an artist it is so important to get your brand down 100%. You want to make sure you have a catchy logo, high-quality photos, website, and social media banners that match. Be extremely intentional with your overall brand. From what outfits you choose to have in your photos, the fonts and colors to use in your collaterals, all the way down to the logo design. Figure out what brand you want to portray then take action steps to make it happen. Look at your favorite artists' websites and social media pages for inspiration.

Things to pay attention to:

- Website

- Photos

- Logo

- Bio

- High-quality song production

- Album cover artwork

All of these will help the music industry, as a whole, take you seriously.

Getting Clear on Your Vision

Close your eyes and visualize your biggest dreams coming true. What would it look like? Who would be next to you? Is it you doing an acceptance speech for a Grammy? Is it live shows? Is it getting your song in that movie? Is it finding that perfect team to work with? Write it down. Make a list of what you want and just start visualizing every day on it.

Now start taking action steps towards it. Write out how you would feel when this happens. Write how you are feeling in the present that this has happened. Go into detail. Future journal. Imagine that amount of money coming into your bank account. What would you do with it? Make a list of things you would buy and how you would spend it. Would you buy new guitars or mics? Would you give it to your family? Would you buy friends an expensive holiday gift? Would you use it to hire high-end marketing or production teams? Ask yourself what do you want? Now go for it!

Keep dreaming. Keep taking action. Keep visualizing.

What do you want? Claim it. Own it. Ask the universe for it. Co-create it. Thank the universe or God for it coming into your life. Get into the feeling of having it.

This Chapter Is Sponsored By

RKV Enterprises LLC
www.linktr.ee/RkvEntertainment

Chapter 12

Think Bigger. You're Playing Too Small

The following information about the three worlds I have learned from the incredible coaches: Genevieve Rackham, Sara Longoria, Jourdan Rystrom, Melanie Ann Layer, Christy Avis, Jess Quigley, Meg Zeek, Jasmine Marra, Kate Decker, Gabriele Weber and anyone else they learned it from. I felt so unbelievably inspired by this perspective that I felt so called to share it with you! In 2020, I kept myself busy by enrolling in a ton of spiritual business courses. I dived deep into metaphysics, the energy of money, and so much more. These worlds are not physical locations. It's about the quantum field, where literally everything is possible.

I believe there are different worlds you can live in. I believe we are all made of energy and therefore, we can bring into our lives that which we focus on, mostly what our subconscious mind is programmed to focus on. This takes time, this is not easy, this requires constant practice. We have to constantly remind ourselves about the world we want to live in. Meaning, we have to constantly remind ourselves to be self-aware and consistently focus on what reality we want to see in our lives.

This does not mean we have control over others, we do not. But we can choose what we focus on and pay attention to the most, and what we intend for our lives and the world. We can always decide to choose how we react to people, places, and circumstances. Do we want to let that person who beeped at us on the highway, ruin our day, or we can choose to let it go? Do we want to let that person we cared about who stopped texting, affect how we feel about ourselves? Or we can choose a different perspective, that maybe that person was just not meant to be our person, maybe the universe or God has a better plan for us! An even better person, or opportunity, or job, etc.

Now, a lot of us live in the victim mentality. We choose to blame others, but when we take radical responsibility for our lives, that is when things can shift drastically. That is when we start taking our power back. That is when we can start having a new perspective and live in the world of possibility and potentiality and attract miracles into our lives! When we take back control of our lives. When we decide what to focus on, what we listen to, what we write about, what we speak, and more.

When you operate out of what's logical for you to earn or to happen, you will only gain logical results. If you do not want logical results, but incredible results, focus on what is possible and not just what is logical. I am here for the people who want to achieve the greatest possible results in their career. Who will go all-in for themselves. Who will jump out of their comfort zone to create space for new opportunities despite their fears.

As soon as people step into my world and invest in themselves, something really powerful happens. Opportunities come out of nowhere, they attract new clients and people to help them. It is so wild what happens when you take action towards your dreams and work with the right people who hold space for you. Literally, anything you want to do is possible. So stop telling yourself it's not realistic or logical. If you only operate from logic, you cut off so many big possibilities. Because the truth is, you have just the same amount of chance of success as you do of failure. So why not lean into what is possible when you dream?

If you are looking to really amplify your career to the next level and you want to learn the information I've learned from women who bring in $100,000 sales a month in their business based on the energetics, who they are, action steps, strategy, confidence, self-awareness, and more. If you want to finally step into your passion and do the scary thing because you know it's going to take your career to the next level. If you want to finally get out of your own way and step into all the dreams you ever imagined by having someone break it down one step at a time. If you want to take your career to the next level, book a call here: www.calendly.com/danifeltcall

Play in Possibilities

Whatever you want to do in your career, it is possible.

- It only takes one key person to open up doors and connect you to who you need.

- It only takes one manager to believe in you and sign you to their firm.

- It only takes one A&R to sign you to a label, sync agency, or publisher.

- It only takes one song that you write to win a Grammy.

- It only takes one person to co-write a song that wins a Grammy or lands in a film or TV show.

It all starts with you. It all starts with taking a chance. It all starts with knocking on every door you find that you feel makes sense and feels good. It all starts with sending that email. It all starts with making that call, or sending out that text, or setting up that coffee meeting. It is all possible. Anything is possible.

Go take action and watch what happens. Never let anyone tell you that you can't go for your dreams. Never let anyone stop you from being happy. Never give any of your power to someone else by staying upset, sad, frustrated, etc. Your power lies in you, inside your mind, heart, and soul. Stay focused. Stay happy. Stay aligned.

Align yourself with people who have your best interest at heart and share your values. Take all the chances. Your thoughts have power, choose them wisely. If you do not believe something is possible, it will not be. If you believe something is possible, it can be. Anything is possible, I repeat, anything is possible. It starts with you—your emotions, your thoughts, your mindset, your beliefs, your actions.

If anyone tells you not to go for your dreams, tell them to F* off. Better yet, just block them, ignore them, don't talk to them, avoid speaking to them as much as you can. Who you surround yourself with is key. What you focus on is key. What action step you take is key. Going for your dreams can be terrifying. Taking the chances, being vulnerable, it can be scary as F*ck. I hear you, I do. But I encourage you to do it anyway, even if it scares the h*ll out of you, freaking go for it, anyway! You never know until you try.

The Three Worlds

So there is the world of logic, the world of possibilities, and the world of potentiality. The world of logic is only logical results, a + b = c. The world of possibilities is playing with what is possible. The last world is the world of potentiality. This is the quantum where everything is possible! This is where the biggest miracles happen and you are left stunned, amazed, and in tears. Let me give you an example so you can understand the difference between each of the worlds.

Logical world: You are going to publish a book and say you have a hundred clients, 10% of those clients could read your book. That is the logical way to see things. After you reach out to a hundred people, maybe 10% of them will book a call with you and then another 10% will purchase from you, that's the rule of 10%. That is one way to look at it.

Another example: You create a TV show concept and you try to find an agent because you are told that is the way to get in the door. Another example: You release a single and because you only have a hundred followers on your Instagram, you think they are the only people who will hear your song.

Another example: You decide to open a coaching business. You see that people are charging $100 per session. So you tell yourself, you can only get paid $100 per call, and so you offer four calls a month and tell yourself you can make $400 a month because that is realistic.

Okay here comes the fun part! Now I want to invite you to play in the world of possibility.

World of possibilities: What if instead of just 10% of your clients read your book, 30% decide to read your book! So maybe 30% of them book a call with you and then 30% purchase from you. Say also, maybe their friends each tell one friend, now you have even more people knowing about your book!

World of possibilities: You create a TV show concept and you decide to go to a networking event and meet a producer that wants to work with you. Now you have a producer who wants to collaborate with you and build the show with you, without having to go find an agent! It is so possible.

World of possibilities: You release a single and you think only your followers on Instagram will hear it. However, each of those one hundred followers decide to share your song and now you have two hundred people that know about your music! Double what you assumed would happen in the logical world.

World of possibilities: You decide to open up a coaching business and instead of charging by the hour you decide to charge what you actually want, maybe it's $1,000 a month. You go to one networking event and meet twenty people and out of those people, five of them book a call with you. Out of those five people, two hire you. Boom! You now have $2,000 a month coming your way. It is possible!

Okay here is the best part! Now it is time to play in the quantum field! The world where literally everything is possible!

World of potentiality: This time, all your one hundred clients decide to purchase your book. Think big! Each of the one hundred clients who purchased the book shared it with one of their friends, and now you have two hundred people that purchased your book!

The producer you met at a party happens to be one of the most successful people in TV. They happen to love your idea and tell you they are going to pitch it to Netflix. Your show becomes one of the most successful TV shows of the year. Now every producer in town is calling you to work with them.

World of potentiality: You release a single, an A&R, and a music licensing agency hears it and contacts you. They decide to sign you to their sync agency and one year later, they get your song featured in a movie trailer for a major picture film in theatres. You receive $50,000 for your song for the movie trailer.

World of potentiality: You open up a coaching business. You go to an event to meet business owners. You meet a business owner who happens to have a lot of money to spend just not enough time. She decides to hire you to help her run her business and be her coach for one year. She decides to pay you $100,000 for the year. Think bigger.

Now it is your turn! Start writing out a list of things you want to bring into your life. Now write out the logical scenario, what would happen in the world of possibilities and the world of potentiality.

Goal 1:

Logical thing that could happen:

World of possibilities that could happen:

World of potentiality that could happen:

Logical thing that could happen:

World of possibilities that could happen:

World of potentiality that could happen:

Goal 2:

Logical thing that could happen:

World of possibilities that could happen:

World of potentiality that could happen:

Logical thing that could happen:

World of possibilities that could happen:

World of potentiality that could happen:

Goal 3:

Logical thing that could happen:

World of possibilities that could happen:

World of potentiality that could happen:

Logical thing that could happen:

World of possibilities that could happen:

World of potentiality that could happen:

Goal 4:

Logical thing that could happen:

World of possibilities that could happen:

World of potentiality that could happen:

Logical thing that could happen:

World of possibilities that could happen:

World of potentiality that could happen:

Goal 5:

Logical thing that could happen:

World of possibilities that could happen:

World of potentiality that could happen:

Logical thing that could happen:

World of possibilities that could happen:

World of potentiality that could happen:

Goal 6:

Logical thing that could happen:

World of possibilities that could happen:

World of potentiality that could happen:

Logical thing that could happen:

World of possibilities that could happen:

World of potentiality that could happen:

Goal 7:

Logical thing that could happen:

World of possibilities that could happen:

World of potentiality that could happen:

Logical thing that could happen:

World of possibilities that could happen:

World of potentiality that could happen:

Goal 8:

Logical thing that could happen:

World of possibilities that could happen:

World of potentiality that could happen:

Logical thing that could happen:

World of possibilities that could happen:

World of potentiality that could happen:

Goal 9:

Logical thing that could happen:

World of possibilities that could happen:

World of potentiality that could happen:

Logical thing that could happen:

World of possibilities that could happen:

World of potentiality that could happen:

Goal 10:

Logical thing that could happen:

World of possibilities that could happen:

World of potentiality that could happen:

Logical thing that could happen:

World of possibilities that could happen:

World of potentiality that could happen:

This Chapter Is Sponsored By

Andi Jane & the Honky Tonk Cabaret
www.andijane.com

Chapter 13

Next Steps (Because Insight Without Action Is Just Vibes)

So now you know what you want to do and you are making a plan of action. You have a new powerful story about yourself and you are ready to dive deep into your dreams and build success for yourself!

Now you have two options. You can continue to figure out the rest on your own or you can bring on people to help you accomplish your dreams. I would love to invite you to book a call with me so I can learn about your goals and see how my team can best help you. Over thirteen years, I have built a full team of incredible people—professional web designers, branding experts, social media managers, celebrity stylists, social media advertising experts, photographers, videographers, graphic designers, business mentors, and more. Whatever it is that you want to accomplish, I can help you!

Book a call today by emailing dani@danifelt.com. You can also schedule a time here: www.calendly.com/danifeltcall/free-consultation-music-industry-mastery. Let's chat!

Thank you for reading this book and taking a powerful step towards your dreams! I'd love for you to keep going and join me on "The Dani Felt Podcast" on Spotify and connect with me on Instagram @danifeltinspires, so you can continue turning inspiration into action.

I hope to hear from you soon!

This Chapter Is Sponsored By

LTI Business Solutions
www.ltibusinesssolutions.com

ACKNOWLEDGMENTS

My dad for always pushing me to be better.
My mom for always encouraging me to go for my dreams.
My sister for always loving me unconditionally.
My brother for always sharing his spiritual mindset with me.
Gabriele Weber for being my intuitive and healer since high school.

Thank you to all my amazing sponsors. You know who you are! I could not have done this without your support. I will forever be grateful.

Thank you to all my former business partners.

Robert Biehn for co-writing and developing a TV show with me.

Steve Owens for mentoring me on TV show development and how to pitch.

Wileen Charles for mentoring me on TV show development.

All the coaches who I worked with one-on-one or purchased their courses or group programs or attended their free webinars: Christy Avis, Kate Decker, Kat Cozadd, Meg Zeek, Jasmine Marra, Melanie Ann Layer, Jourdan Rystrom, Sara Longoria, Jessica Quigley, Coach Rob, Chris Fern, Dylan Gigliotti and Gabriele Weber.

Evan Stein for helping reignite a passion within me to pursue my music again and inspiring me to move to LA.

My good friend Sebastian Rivera, for always supporting me and introducing me to so many people.

Dallas Jack, a close friend and respected peer, for his support, encouragement, and perspective throughout this process, and for writing the Foreword to this book.

My good friend Nicole de la Cruz, for always believing in me and inspiring me to be better.

My colleagues at the University of New Haven and New England School of Communication, and all my professors there.

Jeremy Mathison and The Performance Plus Camp for helping me learn how to write and record music as a teenager.

All my middle school and high school bullies who pushed me to become so much greater.

My music co-writers and producers: Michael Galgano, Zac Lavender, Alethea Buchal, Sebastian Rivera, Ernie Lee, David Dones, LOCS, Jason Threm, Zachary Bourne, Dallas Jack, Grant Woell, Danny Nagy, and John X.

The amazing Kidtee Hello Photography who provided the photography for the cover.

My publishing team, Heather Andrews and Manita Ramos at 27 Degrees Publishing.

All my amazing clients and everyone I work with on my team!

Thank you also to all my amazing friends! Too many of you to name!

ABOUT THE AUTHOR

Dani Felt is a recognized force in music, media, and creative consulting. She is known for helping artists and visionaries transform their passion into purpose-driven, sustainable careers. With over thirteen years of industry experience, Dani has worked across music, TV, branding, and business strategy, guiding creatives at every stage to step confidently into their spotlight.

An active singer-songwriter herself, Dani brings a rare blend of artistic intuition and strategic expertise to her work. Her career began from the inside out as she navigated the challenges, confusion, and emotional highs and lows of the music industry firsthand. Through that journey, she recognized a gap. There were not enough heart-centered consultants who truly understood what creatives needed, not just professionally but personally.

That realization became her mission. Dani went on to curate entertainment showcases and build a career as a trusted consultant, focused on clarity, authenticity, and long-term impact. Her work centers on helping individuals reconnect with who they are, articulate their vision, and build meaningful relationships that move their careers forward.

Dani is known for her instinct, leadership, and ability to see potential before others do. Through customized branding experiences and creative consulting, she helps artists amplify their voice, align their image, and confidently take up space in their industry. At the core of Dani's work is a single guiding belief. When creatives are deeply aligned with who they truly are, clarity follows, opportunities expand, and success becomes possible.

Let's stay connected on socials:

www.instagram.com/danifeltinspires

Learn more about Music Industry Mastery at:

www.caliconnector.com

www.linktr.ee/danifelt